SHILDON TO STOCKTON

The Stockton & Darlington Railway

Roger Darsley and Dennis Lovett

# Middleton Press

Front cover: The Locomotion *replica leads the cavalcade for the S&DR 150 year celebrations on 31st August 1975. The replica was built by Locomotive Enterprises, their no. 1 in 1975. (R.Goad/Armstrong Railway Photographic Trust - ARPT)*

Back cover, lower: A rather romantic view of Corporation Quay and the River Tees at Stockton on 15th January 1966. (J.Boyes/NERA)

Back cover, upper: Railway Clearing House map (edited), dated 1947. The route of the album is shown with a dotted line.

Readers of this book may be interested in the following societies and museums:

North Eastern Railway Association: *www.ner.org.uk*

Railway Correspondence and Travel Society, NE Branch: *darlington@rcts.org.uk*

Industrial Railway Society: *www.irsociety.co.uk*

Locomotion (Shildon): *www.locomotion.org.uk*

A1 Steam Locomotive Trust: *www.a1steam.com*

Hopetown Darlington - North Road Railway Museum (formerly Head of Steam):
https://www.hopetowndarlington.co.uk/

Darlington Railway Preservation Society: *www.drps.synthasite.com*

North Eastern Locomotive Preservation Group: *https://nelpg.org/*

Friends of the Stockton & Darlington Railway: *www.sdr1825.org.uk*

Published August 2023
First reprint June 2025

ISBN 978 1 910356 79 1

© Middleton Press Ltd, 2023

Cover design and Photographic enhancement Deborah Esher
Production Cassandra Morgan

Published by
    Middleton Press Ltd
    Camelsdale Road
    Haslemere
    Surrey
    GU27 3RJ
Tel: 01730 813169
Email: info@middletonpress.co.uk
www.middletonpress.co.uk

Printed by 4Bind Ltd, Unit B Caxton Point, Caxton Way, Stevenage, Hertfordshire SG1 2XU
Telephone +44 (0) 1438 745005; www.4bind.co.uk

SECTIONS

1. Beyond Shildon	1-10
2. Shildon, the first railway town	11-34
3. Shildon to North Road	35-69
4. North Road to Oak Tree Junction via Fighting Cocks	70-75
5. North Road to Croft via Darlington Bank Top	76-87
6. Darlington South Junction to Oak Tree Junction via Dinsdale	88-91
7. Oak Tree Junction to Yarm and Stockton	92-120

CONTENTS

95	Allens West	102	Eaglescliffe	23	Shildon
5	Butterknowle	73	Fighting Cocks	107	Stockton
86	Croft	39	Heighington	92	Teesside Airport
80	Darlington Bank Top	36	Newton Aycliffe	98	Yarm (S&DR)
88	Dinsdale	64	North Road	98-101	Yarm Branch

ACKNOWLEDGEMENTS

We are grateful for the assistance received from many of those mentioned in the photographic credits and to A. Coulls, G. Croughton, G. Gartside, C.M. Howard, N. Langridge, A. McLean, J. Midcalf (ARPT), B. Read, D. and Dr S. Salter, M. Stewart, D. Tyreman, J.P. Vickers, J.W. Yellowlees and A.E. Young.

I. A map of the lines covered in this album are shown in solid black. (Middleton Press)

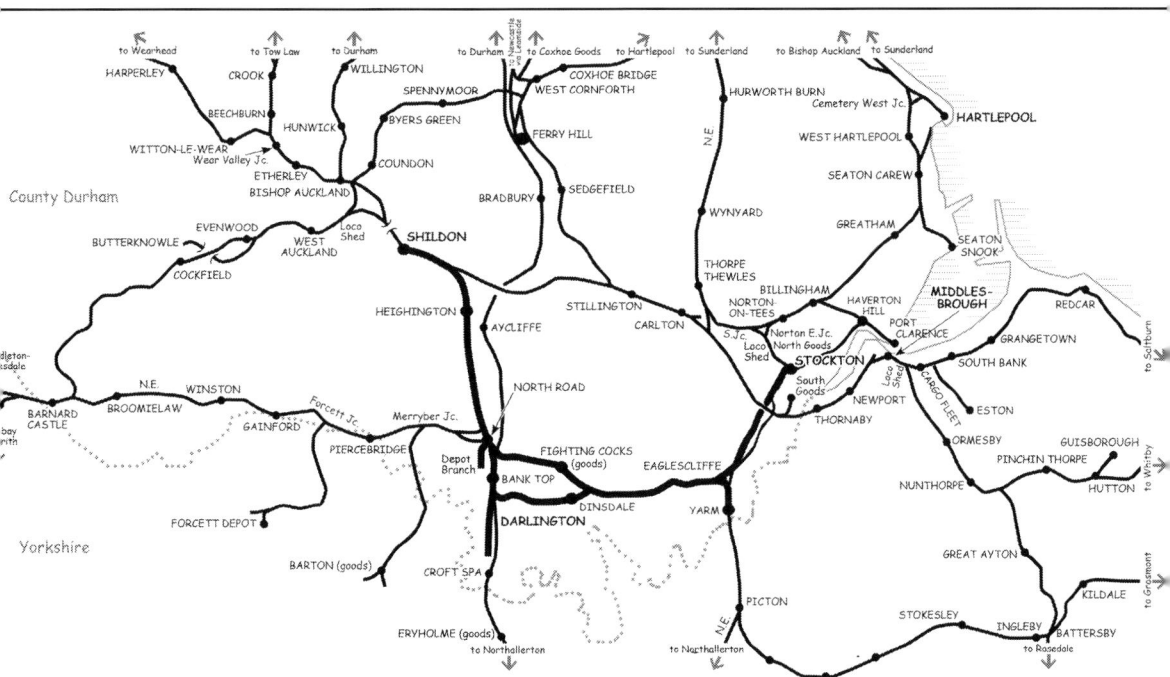

GEOGRAPHICAL SETTING

The area to the north and west of Darlington sits on the edge of the Pennines. The Shildon area was a major supplier of coal before World War One (WWI, 1914-18) although other minerals such as iron ore and limestone were extracted as well. To the north of Shildon lies Weardale, which would later see rails laid in the valley of the River Wear. Coal and ironstone were needed to fuel the steel industry that evolved around Middlesbrough, whilst coal fed the mills and foundries of Darlington. Likewise, the shipbuilding and iron manufacturers initially used locally sourced iron ore.

To the east of Darlington, the line follows the Tees Valley until it reaches Stockton which was the initial point for unloading coal into coastal ships. It was, however, soon realised that moving the transhipment point to what is now Middlesbrough nearer to the mouth of the river, would enable bigger ships and larger loads to be carried. The Tees is fed by several rivers including the River Skerne, which flows through Darlington and was made famous by Dobbin's painting of the opening of the Stockton & Darlington Railway (S&DR) that depicts the inaugural train crossing the S&DR bridge over the river. The Skerne flows into the Tees three miles east of Darlington. The Tees also flows through the southern part of Darlington and forms the boundary between County Durham and North Yorkshire.

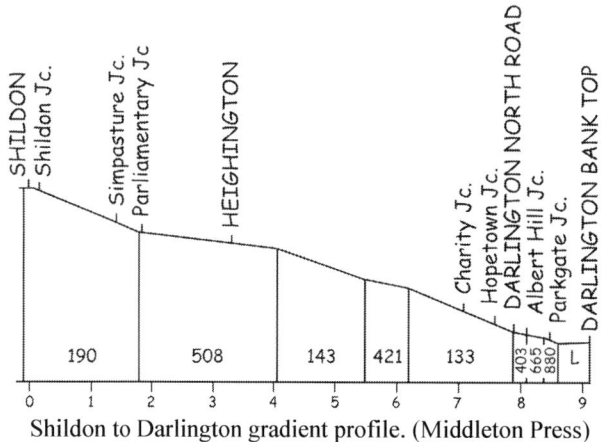

Shildon to Darlington gradient profile. (Middleton Press)

HISTORICAL BACKGROUND

There have probably been more words written about the S&DR than any other railway anywhere in the world. Many will be surprised to find that it did not run just between the two towns after which it takes its name but was built to bring coal down to the River Tees from the Shildon area, some 17 ½ miles away, from where it could be loaded onto coastal shipping. Its title was down to who provided the money, and it was the promoters from both towns who provided the bulk of it. Shildon at the time was little more than a village with the mining output in the area being modest and almost impossible to transport in anything but small quantities.

It was not the first railway to be built nor the first to have steam haulage. These were mostly confined to colliery or mineral lines and waggonways, some of which could be traced back to the 17th century in the northeast. Where the S&DR differed was that it was a public railway allowing anyone's goods or themselves to be transported from day one upon payment of the appropriate fees. It was this that kick-started the railway revolution, not just at home but across the world.

Although its title may suggest a harmonious agreement between the two towns, the initial plans centred around the construction of a canal. Such a scheme had been promoted as early as 1813 when John Rennie surveyed the route and recommended its suitability for canal construction. Edward Pease, a Darlington mill owner, counter-proposed that a railway should be built to bring the coal from Shildon to the River Tees and to ensure that the industry in Darlington benefitted from the reduction in coal prices that would result. Stockton wanted a similar route to the proposed canal but on a more northerly route which bypassed both Darlington and Yarm. Not surprisingly, business owners in both towns were not supportive and as much of the finance was being provided from those areas this was not an option that was considered satisfactory to them.

The proposed line was first surveyed by George Overton in 1818 but it was George Stephenson, already well known in the northeast for his development of the colliery line at Killingworth and later the Hetton Colliery Railway, both of which were early users of steam locomotives, who carried out the final survey. It was Stephenson who persuaded Edward Pease and his co-directors to opt for steam power rather than using horses to pull the trucks.

Having secured the parliamentary bill in 1821, construction began the same year following Stephenson's survey, which was carried out in the company of his 18-year-old son Robert, who would become as well-known as his father in developing the early railway network and building steam locomotives through his Newcastle based company.

Not long after the S&DR had opened on 27th September 1825 from Witton Park Colliery to Stockton, it faced competition from a new line, the Clarence Railway, opened in 1833. The new route was just 11½ miles long and, after the opening of the main line between Darlington and Newcastle in 1844, was not impaired by having to cross that new line on the level as the S&DR did, on a flat crossing ('S&D Crossing') at Darlington; the Clarence line was carried above it on an overbridge just north of Aycliffe. The S&DR, however, fed this new railway at Simpasture and could charge a tariff for the transit of coal trucks over its own line, which made it more expensive to move traffic over the new line than by the S&DR route, which was longer.

The S&DR was a pioneering operation and could not draw on the experience of other such lines. As a coal carrier it gave little thought initially to passenger traffic and franchised passenger operations to private coach operators who used horsepower to work a section of line allocated to them. Regular passenger services commenced between Stockton and Darlington on 10th October 1825, extended to Shildon from April 1826 and over the Yarm branch from 16th October 1826, this latter mostly served by Stockton to Darlington trains making a detour along the branch and back. The S&DR eventually began to buy out the private operators from 7th September 1833 when it introduced steam-hauled passenger services between Stockton and Darlington, extended to Shildon and St. Helen's (later renamed West Auckland) in December 1833.

Stations were not provided initially, the coaches stopping at nearby inns, which also provided limited passenger comforts in the form of waiting rooms and booking offices. The Masons Arms in Shildon was the first terminus in Shildon and this was later changed for The Grey Horse Inn, which happened to be owned by the operator of the coach service to Darlington! Coaches could of course stop anywhere enroute to pick up or drop off passengers as dedicated station facilities that we take for granted today had yet to be conceived. The early stopping places were mostly where the line crossed roads, for example Aycliffe Lane, Fighting Cocks, Goosepool, Yarm (location of the present Allens West station) and at the end of the Yarm branch.

Fighting Cocks was served by a nearby inn of the same name, whilst, in Stockton, trains terminated at The Railway Tavern built by the S&DR. The company also built inns at North Road in Darlington and at Heighington for the same purposes, all of which remain in use as public houses today.

The North Eastern Railway (NER) was formed in 1854 by amalgamation of the Leeds & Thirsk Railway, Leeds Northern Railway, Malton & Driffield Junction Railway, York & North Midland Railway and the York, Newcastle & Berwick Railway. The NER took over the S&DR in 1863 by which time the latter company owned some 200 route miles, embracing routes over the Pennines to Tebay (Westmorland), Penrith (Cumberland) as well as across vast swathes of County Durham from Weardale to the east coast at Saltburn. This allowed some of the early depots to be replaced by new facilities to meet the needs of an expanding NER empire.

From 1st July 1887, passenger services over the former S&DR were re-routed through Darlington Bank Top station. This opened on the same day, utilising a new line, from Darlington South Junction to Oak Tree Junction, which also opened on this day with Dinsdale station replacing Fighting Cocks on the old route. At Oak Tree Junction the trains re-joined the original route, which was retained for freight services but also saw some excursion trains and diverted services. The new route provided interchange facilities with the East Coast Main Line (ECML) at Bank Top and avoided the need to cross the ECML on the level at S&D Crossing by taking the curve from North Road station (Albert Hill Junction) to Parkgate

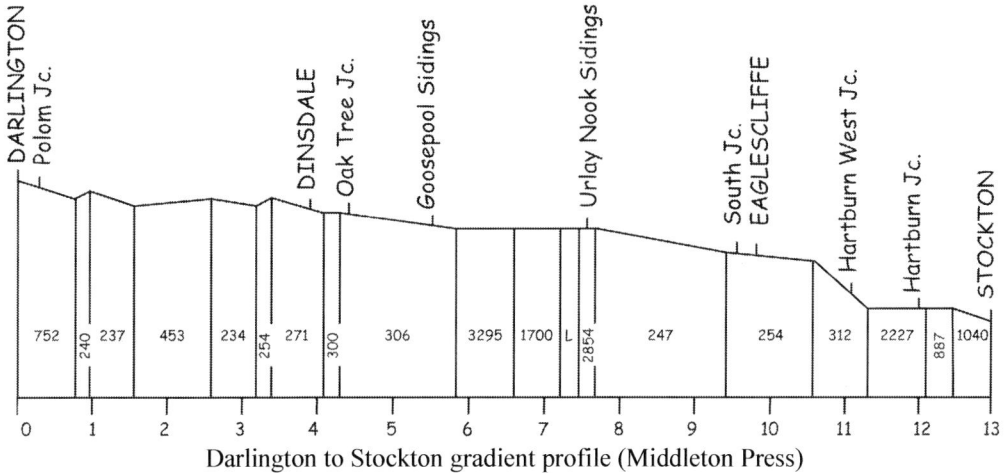

Darlington to Stockton gradient profile (Middleton Press)

Junction. The latter had formed part of the original S&DR route to Croft depot, south of Darlington, opened in 1829. Part of the Croft line was later used for the ECML, opened between York and Darlington by the Great North of England Railway (GNofER) in 1841.

Such was the level of coal traffic from the collieries around Shildon before WWI that it was decided to electrify the line between Shildon and Newport Yard, near Middlesbrough, using the 1,500v DC overhead line system. This included the former Clarence Railway from Simpasture Junction. (Please note, only the section between Shildon and Simpasture Junction is covered by this album.) Electric working was introduced in 1915 but, unfortunately, the post-WWI recession and reducing coal stocks resulted in declining traffic. Extensive renewals of the overhead line equipment were becoming due by the early-1930s, but due to the drop-off in traffic it was decided to abandon electric working and revert to steam haulage, effected in 1935.

The NER became part of the London & North Eastern Railway (LNER) on 1st January 1923 and, upon nationalisation on 1st January 1948, became part of British Railways North Eastern Region and subsequently, from 1st January 1967, British Rail Eastern Region. Following the passing of the Railways Act 1993, services were franchised to the private sector with the ECML through Darlington and the former S&DR line seeing several operators over the years. The ECML was electrified in 1991.

Today the former S&DR routes are known as the Tees Valley Line, east of Darlington, and as the Bishop Line, between Darlington and Bishop Auckland through Shildon.

Large-scale anniversary celebrations were held in 1875, 1925 and 1975. As we fast approach the 200-year mark, events are being planned for 2025. The line will once again be in the spotlight, just as it was when *Locomotion* hauled the first train and ensured that Stockton and Darlington had started a railway revolution that would spread across the entire world.

PASSENGER SERVICES

The 1922 timetable, the last to be issued by the NER, shows nine trains in each direction serving stations at North Road, Heighington and Shildon. These continued or commenced to and from Bishop Auckland, Tow Law or Blackhill. There were two trains on Sundays. There were an additional seven services in each direction between North Road and Darlington Bank Top provided by trains using the Barnard Castle route. There were 18 down trains and 22 up (to Darlington) a day between Darlington Bank Top and Eaglescliffe but not all stopped at Dinsdale.

By 1961 some 20 trains ran between Darlington Bank Top and Crook via Bishop Auckland serving stations to Shildon. Of these, one started at North Road and two of them terminated at Bishop Auckland. Additional trains ran between Darlington Bank Top and North Road, which operated to Penrith. There were 23 up trains to Darlington Bank Top with one early morning service terminating at North Road.

There were 38 down trains in 1961 from Darlington Bank Top to Dinsdale and Eaglescliffe, most of which terminated at Saltburn. A further 38 ran in the opposite direction at half-hour intervals during the day.

Local trains currently operated by Northern run between Saltburn and Bishop Auckland and vice-versa through Middlesbrough and connecting with East Coast Main Line services at Darlington Bank Top. These amount to 15 up trains running an hourly interval service and 13 down trains between Darlington and Bishop Auckland. There is an hourly service on Sundays. ECML services through Darlington are operated by LNER.

Trains east of Darlington are more frequent as Whitby via Middlesbrough services also utilise the S&DR line as far as Eaglescliffe. Eaglescliffe is additionally served by Grand Central services between London King's Cross and Sunderland via Northallerton, whilst TransPennine Express trains between Manchester Airport and Saltburn also pass through Eaglescliffe. There are local Northern services to Stockton, which can be accessed from the S&DR line by changing at Thornaby on to Middlesbrough to Sunderland/Newcastle services.

Freight trains today are of course greatly reduced, with none presently booked to run between Darlington and Bishop Auckland, although the Hitachi Rail Europe factory at Newton Aycliffe (Merchant Park), opened in 2015 with siding access near Heighington, continues to build new passenger rolling stock. Apart from this, there are no other active siding connections between Darlington and Bishop Auckland, except from those associated with preservation activities at both places as detailed in the photo captions. A few long-distance freight services run daily between Darlington and Eaglescliffe, but a greater number pass through the latter station, some en-route from/to Tees Dock and Yard.

1. Beyond Shildon

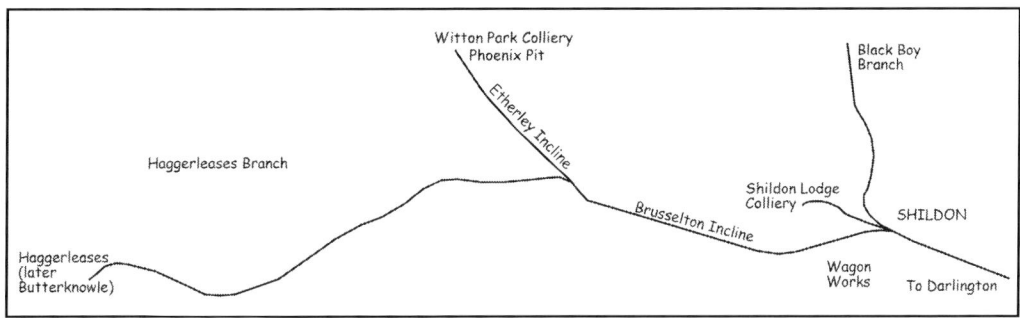

II. Map of railways in the Shildon Area around 1831. (Middleton Press)

The original line to Witton Park Colliery (Phoenix Pit)

The original main line continued some 5 miles beyond Shildon to terminate close to Witton Park Colliery, which was also known as Phoenix Pit. Coal mining had been in the area since 1756 but it was not until the opening of Jane Pit that it became a commercial operation. Several other pits were opened on the site including Mary Ann, George, Corving and William Pits. Transportation of coal to where it was needed was difficult, employing panniers on packhorses, more than trebling the price at Darlington compared with the price at the pithead. This was the driver in the building of the S&DR to remove it in bulk, much more cost-effectively.

From 1845 the pits supplied the Witton Park Iron Works. Whilst limestone could be sourced locally alongside the coal, the iron ore was transported from elsewhere notably the East Midlands. The ironworks closed in 1884 in favour of steel production which was transferred to nearer the coast in what is now Cleveland.

The decline of the collieries coincided with WWI when many miners took to the trenches and diminishing coal seams resulted in the last closure in April 1925 when Jane Pit ceased operation.

The free ticket issued by the Stockton & Darlington company to George Stephenson. The front is seen left, and the reverse, right.

↓ Witton Park to Shildon gradient profile. (Middleton Press)

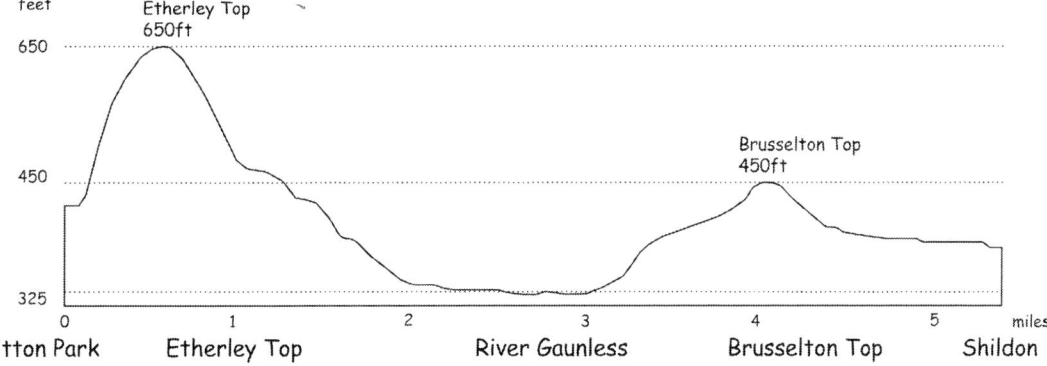

1. The sketches by Thomas Hair of the northeast coal field are well known. This is of St. Helen Auckland. This was the major colliery reached by the Brusselton Incline though the number of collieries grew when the railway started working. The S&DR reached Witton Park via the Etherley Incline. This was not the present Witton Park but a point ½ mile further south. (T.Hair/Tyne & Wear Archives and Museums)

Etherley Incline

From the colliery, coal trucks travelling towards Shildon were raised to the summit of the Etherley Incline and then lowered again using a steam-powered engine house to haul waggons up and down the incline. This remained in use until 1843, rendered redundant and subsequently abandoned, supplanted by the new line northwards through Shildon Tunnel to Bishop Auckland, with Phoenix Pit joined to the system via Fielden Bridge Junction.

Waggons were hauled to the foot of the incline nearest the colliery 1,100 yards up the incline to reach the summit at 650ft and then 2,185 yards distance down the other side towards the Gaunless Bridge at 325ft above sea level. The section between the two inclines was worked by horses. Access to the Haggerleases branch was between the two inclines.

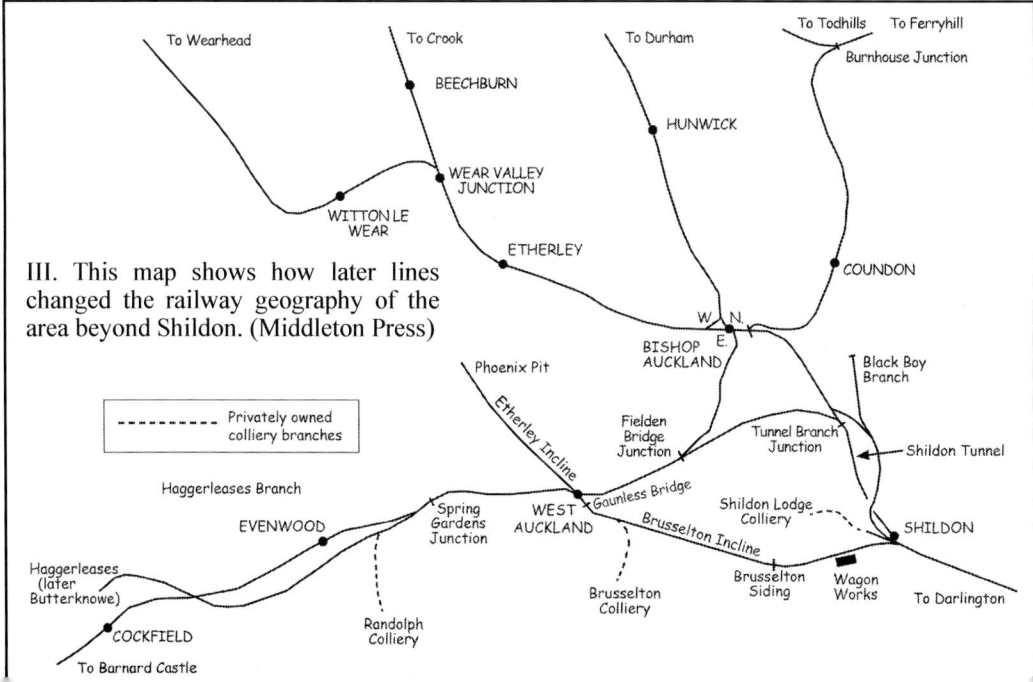

III. This map shows how later lines changed the railway geography of the area beyond Shildon. (Middleton Press)

Gaunless Bridge

Between the two inclines lays the River Gaunless. The river was bridged by the first cast iron railway bridge. Designed by George Stephenson, it was built by John & Isaac Burrell at Newcastle-upon-Tyne, construction commencing in 1823 and was completed in time for the opening in 1825.

Following the construction of alternative routes, which no longer required the use of the inclines, the bridge remained in use on the level section between the inclines that was fed by a new line, the 'Tunnel Branch' from the north end of Shildon Tunnel (Tunnel Branch Junction) to Feildon Bridge Junction, via West Auckland to serve the Butterknowle line (previously known as the Haggerleases branch). This was opened on 13th September 1856 for goods and 13th October 1858 to passengers, bypassing the Brusselton inclines. It was subsequently replaced by a new bridge but because of its historical importance was dismantled and later exhibited at the old York Railway Museum in Queen Street after its opening by the LNER in 1928. It was subsequently re-erected in the grounds of the National Railway Museum at York following its opening in 1975.

As part of the expansion of Locomotion, Shildon, the bridge has been transferred to Shildon where it will be exhibited in time for the 200th Anniversary in 2025.

Brusselton Incline

2. This is an engraving representing the Brusselton Incline. The winding house still exists with a section of the original track on stone sleepers leading to it. Originally it had two 30hp steam engines working the ropes. The operation of the incline was put out to contract and private users paid by weight of goods carried. On reaching the foot of the Brusselton Incline the waggons were connected to the winding house and ascended the line which was 1,960 yards long rising to 450ft to the summit. The waggons then descended on the eastern line some 880 yards with a fall of 90ft.

There is a convention to use the spelling 'waggons' for waggon-ways and 'wagons' for railways; 1825 was a turning point.
(R.Humm coll.)

← 1880 timetable extract when services ran via Fighting Cocks.

3. This a Dandy Car or cart. The horse was carried in this vehicle at the end of a rake of chauldron waggons when not required to pull the waggons. This is probably a replica built by Shildon Wagon works for the S&DR celebrations in 1925. Up to three dandy cars could be attached to a line of waggons. The horses soon learned when to get on and off.
(R.R.Darsley coll.)

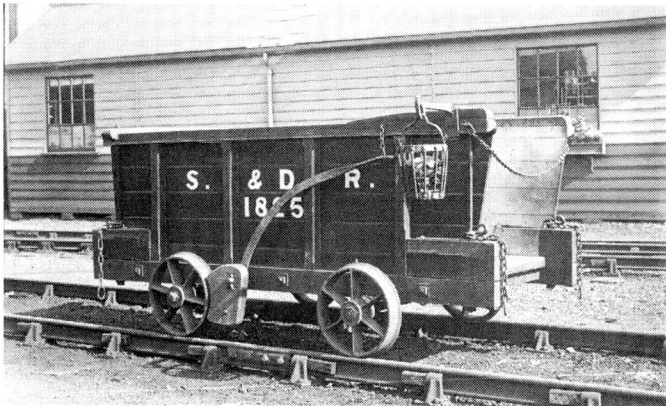

4. We are at the base of the Brusselton Incline in 1932. The NER electrification system finished at the Shildon end of the incline. The incline was made redundant by the 1842 tunnel route but not formally closed until 13th October 1858. Even then it was maintained until the 1880s against possible tunnel blockage.
(W.Rogerson/R.R.Darsley coll.)

BUTTERKNOWLE

Haggerleases (later Butterknowle) branch

The Haggerleases branch left the main line at the bottom of Etherley Incline near St Helen's and served the collieries of the Gaunless Valley. Work on the 5 mile branch began in 1824 although it did not open until 1830. The line terminated at Hagger Leases Lane although it was referred to as Haggerleases and provided access to the collieries at Butterknowle and Copley Bent, the line passing through St. Helen's, Evenwood, Hamsterley and Cockfield en-route.

The line had short-lived passenger services from 24th March 1834 which were horse-drawn and ran from Shildon via St. Helen's (renamed West Auckland from 1st March 1878) to Lands until 1847. From 13th October 1858, services to Lands restarted via the Shildon Tunnel branch, extended to Haggerleases for a short period in 1859. Locomotives were not introduced on to the branch until 1856, freight traffic up until then continuing to Shildon via the Brusselton Incline.

In April 1839 work began on the construction of Shildon Tunnel by the Shildon Tunnel Company. Work was completed on 10th January 1842 with the laying of the last brick. Its opening led in 1856 to the abandonment of the Brusselton incline allowing locomotives to access the Haggerleases branch. Passenger trains thereon ran between 1862 and 1872 only on market days as the South Durham & Lancashire Union Railway (SD&LUR) between Bishop Auckland and Barnard Castle, which opened in 1863, and utilised part of the branch, took much of the traffic with stations provided nearby at Cockfield Fell and Evenwood to serve the local area. The SD&LUR crossed the Haggerleases branch on the tall Gaunless (Lands) viaduct. The branch itself remained goods only and became the Butterknowle branch after 1st September 1899, closing on 30th September 1963.

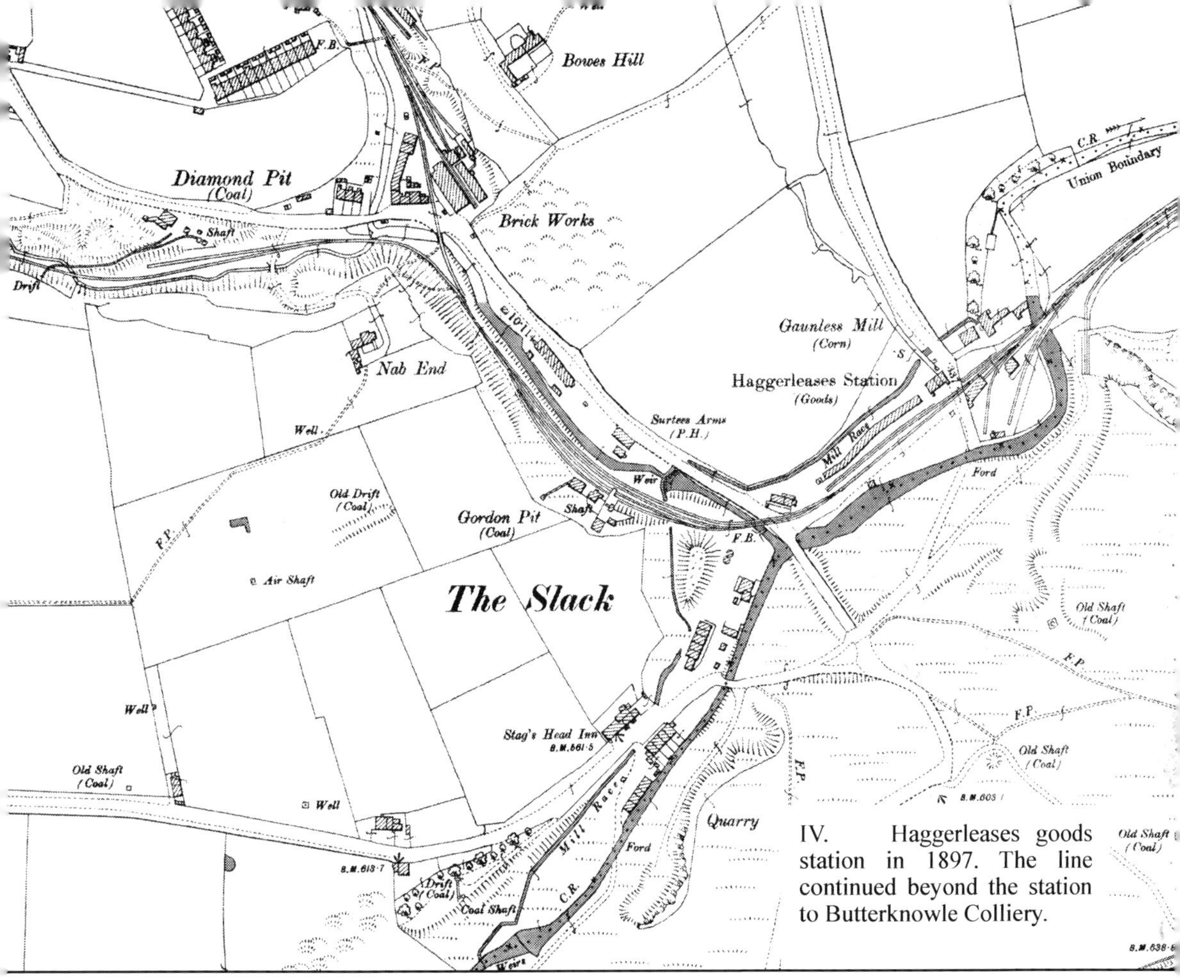

IV. Haggerleases goods station in 1897. The line continued beyond the station to Butterknowle Colliery.

5. The Haggerleases station house has been restored and this was how it looked on 14th July 2004. The branch left from a junction near St. Helen's. A small goods shed and the face of one loading bay also remain. (A.E.Young)

6. This is the 4.9 mile-long branch to Haggerleases on the 9th February 1964. Originally it was horse drawn, single track and with passing places. (R.Goad/ARPT)

Butterknowle Colliery

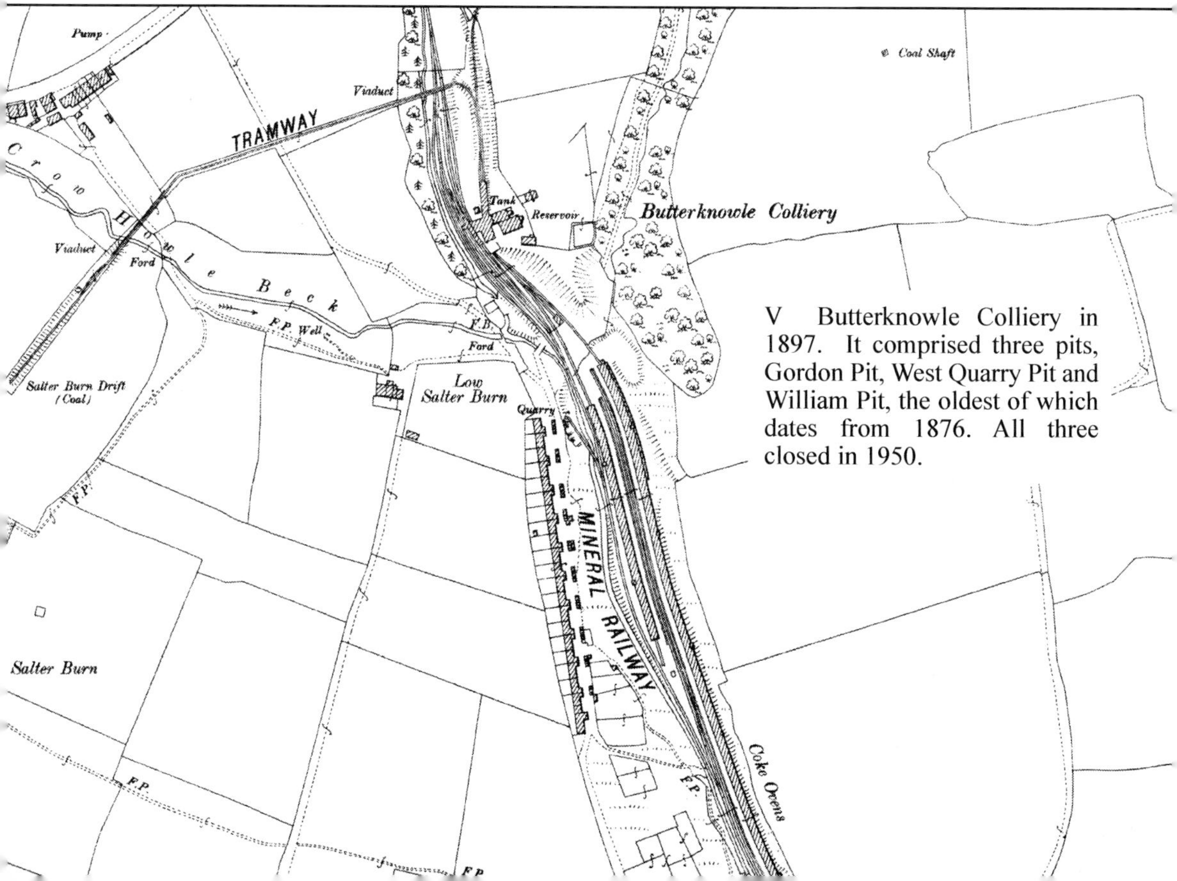

V Butterknowle Colliery in 1897. It comprised three pits, Gordon Pit, West Quarry Pit and William Pit, the oldest of which dates from 1876. All three closed in 1950.

7. Butterknowle Goods Depot at the end of the Haggerleases branch was photographed on 24th January 1965. There was a limited passenger service on the branch to Cockfield, Lands and Butterknowle until 1863. (R.Goad/ARPT)

1922 timetable extract showing services between Darlington North Road and Darlington Bank Top.

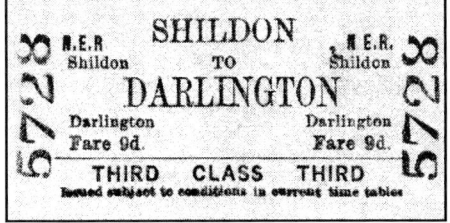

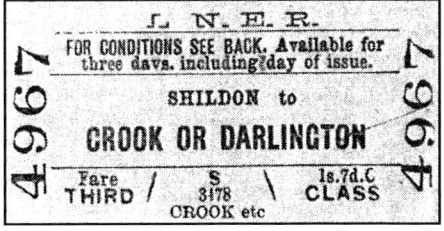

Randolph Colliery (Evenwood Colliery)

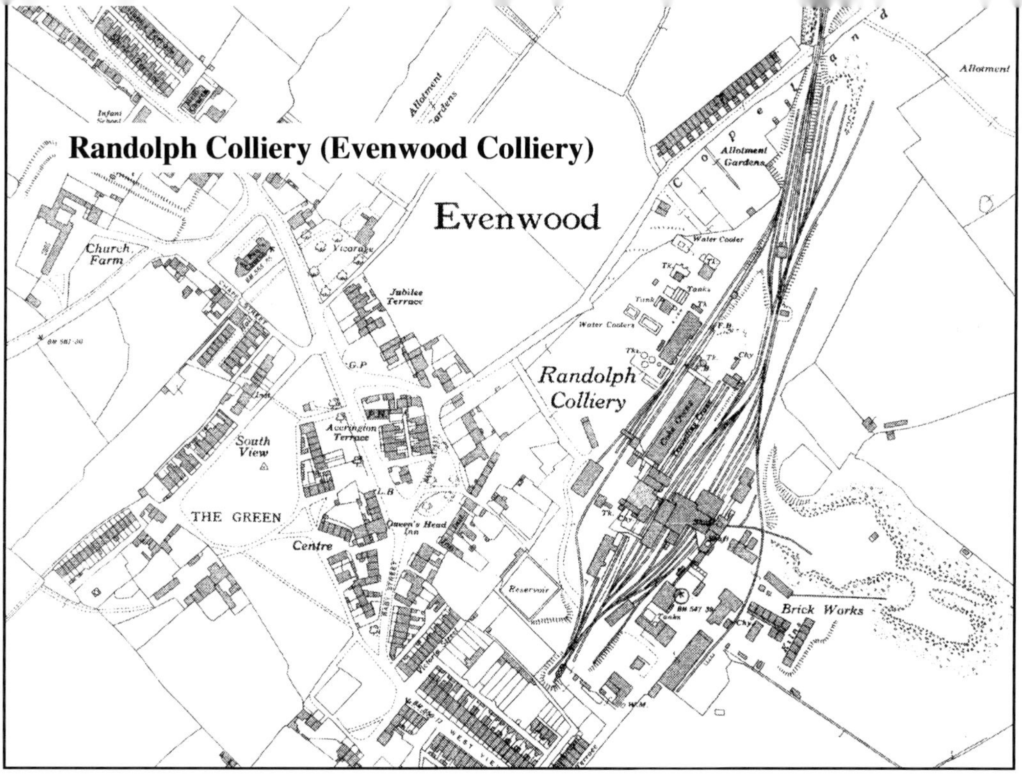

VI. Randolph Colliery, also known as Evenwood Colliery, is seen here in 1943. Opened in 1892, it was served by a branch off the Haggerleases branch.

The North Bitchburn Coal Company purchased Storey Lodge, Evenwood and Thrushwood collieries in 1892 and began sinking Randolph Colliery at Evenwood. Coke ovens were erected in 1895 with more added in 1897, by which time it employed some 500 people producing some 800 tons daily. Randolph Colliery and its coke works were served by an incline worked by a stationary steam engine, which gave access to the Haggerleases branch. Latterly, train loads of coke were despatched to Millom Ironworks via Barnard Castle, Tebay and the West Coast Main Line to Arnside until July 1960.

Randolph Colliery closed on 31st August 1968 leading to closure of the line from Shildon Tunnel Branch Junction the following year.

Brusselton Colliery

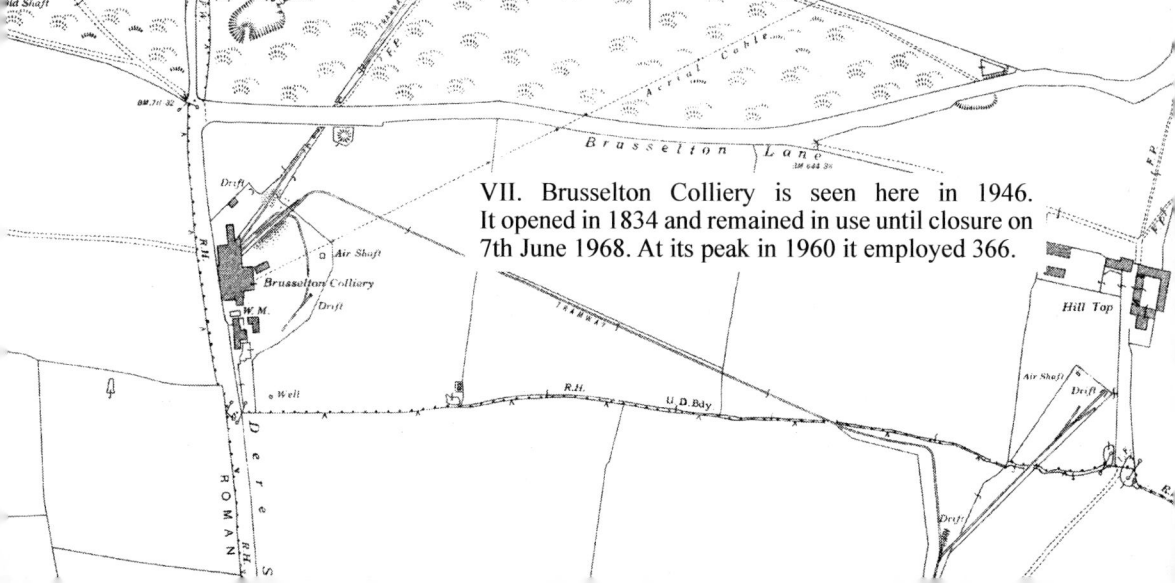

VII. Brusselton Colliery is seen here in 1946. It opened in 1834 and remained in use until closure on 7th June 1968. At its peak in 1960 it employed 366.

Surtees Railway

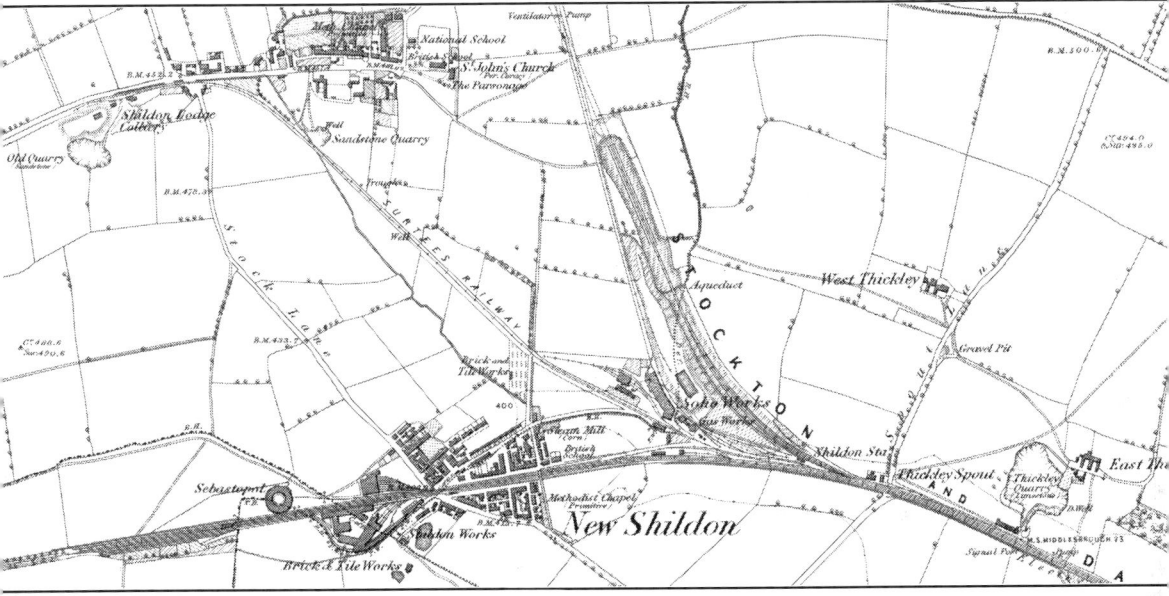

VIII. Surtees branch to Shildon Lodge Colliery is shown on the 6ins to 1 mile map of 1857. This line served Shildon Lodge Colliery which was owned by the Surtees family when it opened in 1830. It closed in 1937. The branch was extended to serve West Durham Wallsend Colliery, opened around 1894 (Wallsend in this context is the type of coal not the place). Land for the line was acquired in 1831 to build the railway from a junction with the lines already open in Shildon.

8. Surtees owned the Shildon Lodge Colliery and built the short branch to connect it to the S&DR. The photographer was facing west at the junction of West Street (now known as West Road) and Auckland Terrace. The branch to Shildon ran behind the fence curving to the south east. The date is similar to that of map IX, overleaf. (J.B.Archive)

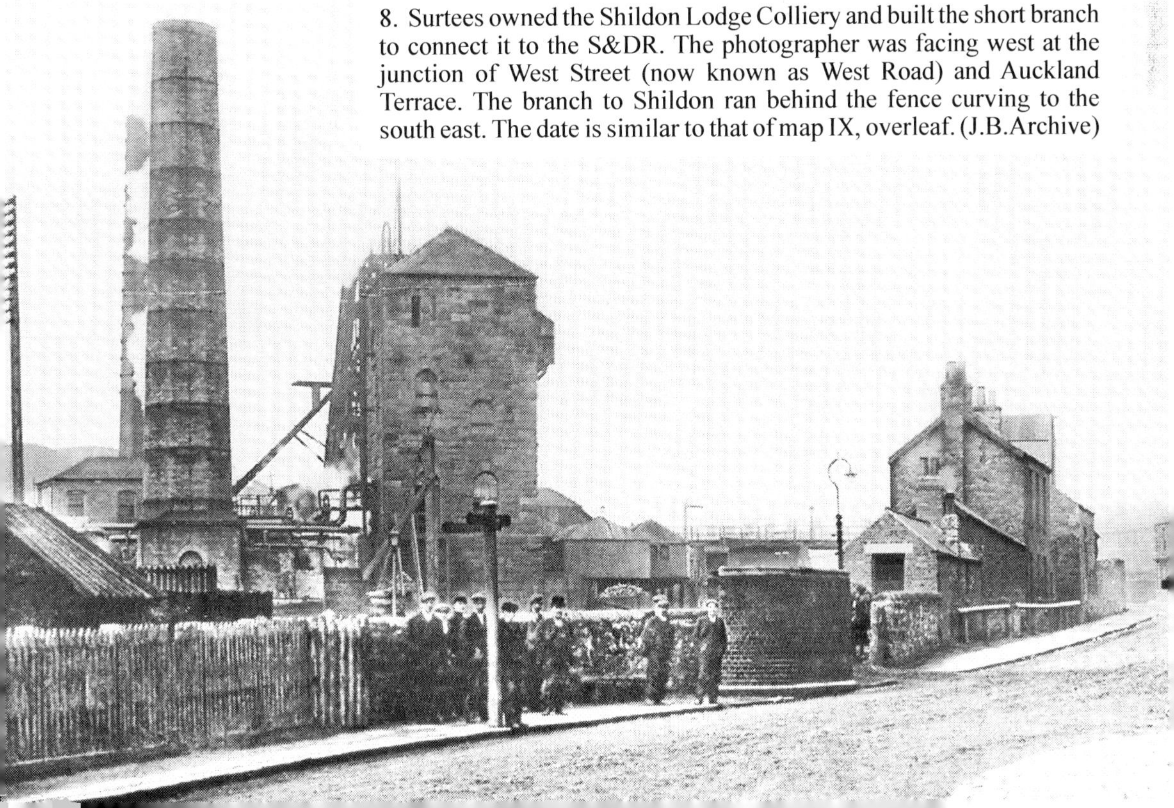

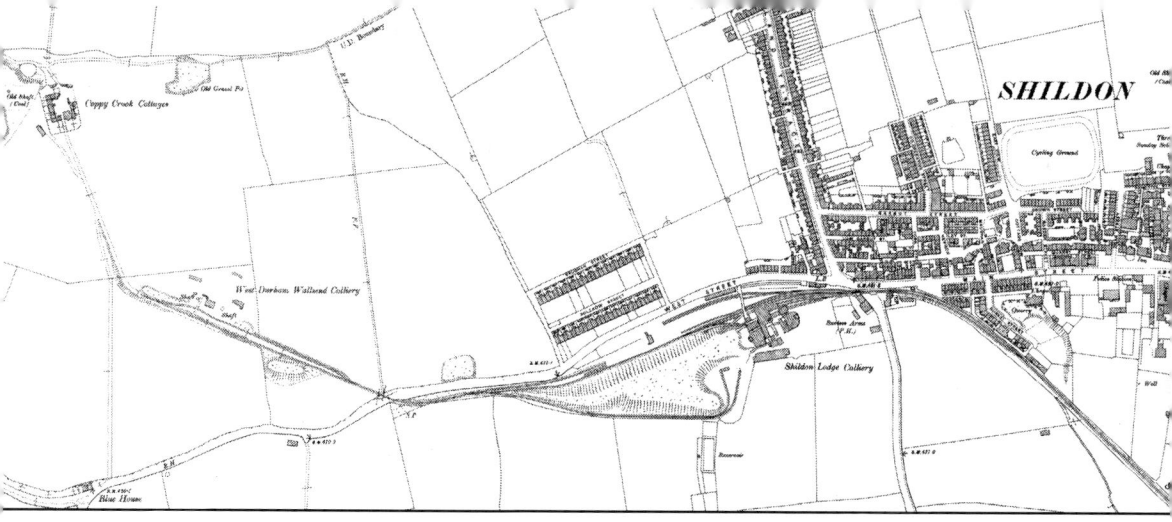

IX. This 1895 extract shows the extension of the Surtees Railway to serve West Durham Wallsend Colliery.

Black Boy branch

X. This is the route of the Black Boy branch seen here in 1896. This 2½ mile long branch line opened on 10th July 1827. The line left the original line near to the Shildon coal drops (which still stand). The Black Boy stables housed the horses which took the waggons up to High Shildon by running through the streets. The climb rises some 500ft above the rapidly expanding railway town before descending into the Dene Valley around the village of Eldon to reach Black Boy Colliery. From the start, the railway was horse-drawn and gravity worked. This changed when a stationary steam engine was installed in 1828 to work the inclines.

Although the colliery was later reached via Shildon Tunnel, part of the branch remained in use until the 1920s to serve a coal depot at the summit.

The origin of the colliery name is uncertain. One theory is that the name came from the hill itself where coal was plentiful. Another is that the colliery was named after the young lads who worked the narrow seams, who, at the end of their shift, emerged covered in coal dust.

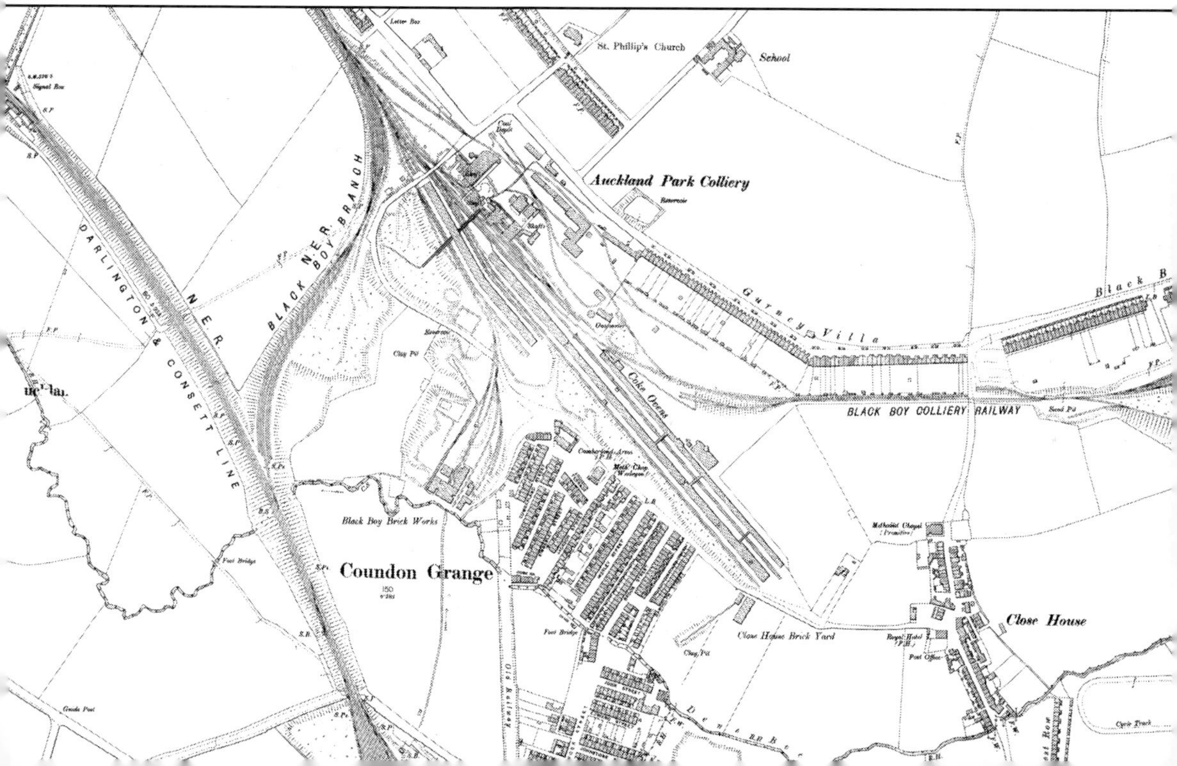

9. Part of the unrestored remains of the early S&DR are the lineside cabins for the horse-drawn Black Boy line at New Shildon. The photograph was taken on 2nd December 2004. (R.R.Darsley)

Adamson's Coach House

Daniel Adamson was the operator of the first passenger service from The Masons Arms, Shildon to Darlington using a coach hauled by a single horse. When the Surtees Railway opened in 1831, he terminated his services at The Grey Horse Inn, which he owned, and constructed a coach house around this time with doors at each end. He was carrying around 74 passengers a week and operating some 12 services per week. Passengers were charged on a per mile basis (as charged for carrying goods) at 1½ old pence for an inside journey and 1 old penny for sitting outside.

10. Daniel Adamson had this coach house at the junction of Main Street and Byerley Road from which he ran the passenger coach, *Perseverance*. The entrance has been blocked up. The photographer was here on 18th September 2013. The historic building was fully restored and formally reopened on 19th June 2002, although the arches through which the coach entered for storage have long been filled in but are still highly visible. (R.Humm)

2. Shildon - the first railway town
Shildon Works & Shed

11. Timothy Hackworth (1786-1850) was a colliery blacksmith and prominent Methodist, who moved to Shildon to take up the post of resident engineer for the S&DR and this is the house built for him. He had his own engineering business and built the locomotive *Sans Pareil* for the Rainhill Trials of 1830. The date of the photograph was 1st November 2000. (R.R.Darsley)

12. Hackworth's Soho Works carried on after his death in 1850 but railway work ceased in 1871 and the works closed in 1883. The main building, seen here, has been demolished but the 1825 engine house at Beamish - Living Museum of the North - is based on this building. This shows the original building in its 1933 condition. (J.W.Armstrong/ARPT)

13. This building is older than the Soho Works but was used as the paint shop. It has been used to store the remains of 0-6-0 *Nelson Bradyll*. Though thought to be built by Hackworth in about 1835, this locomotive may have been built by George Fossick and Thomas Hackworth (Timothy's brother) in Stockton. This is the rear of the building on 3rd December 1967. (J.Boyes/ARPT)

14. A fine collection of stalwart workers from the Soho Works are grouped for their official photograph. (K.Taylor coll./NERA)

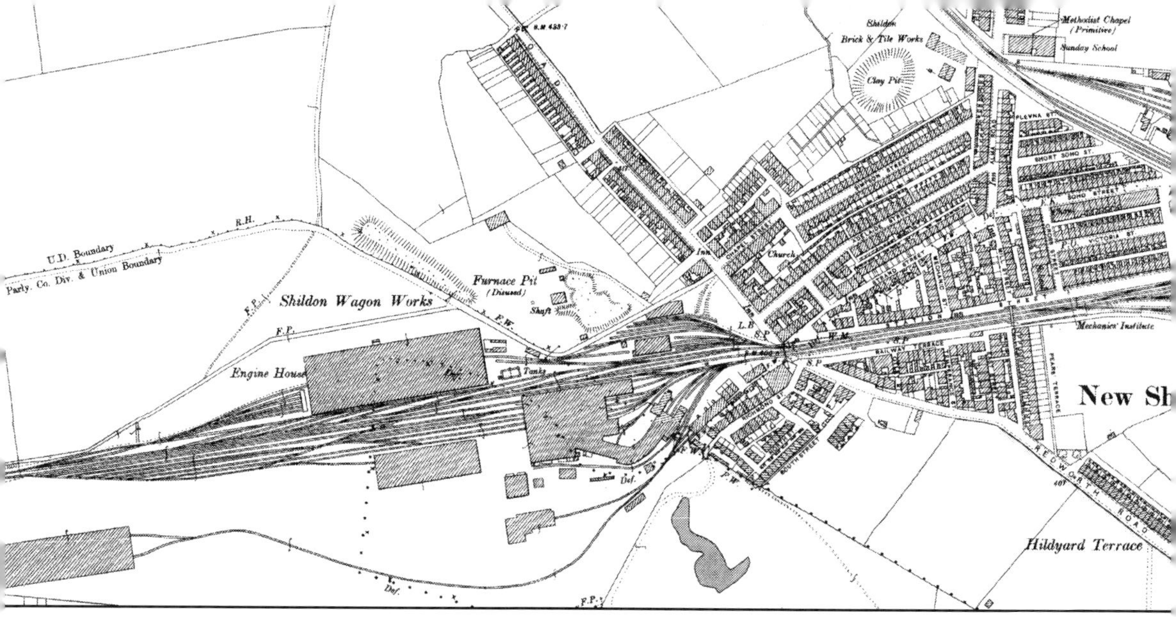

XI. Shildon Works in 1896. The large three turntable engine shed is shown as the Engine House on the map. The Shildon Loco works had opened in 1833 on a new site as the original Soho Works were now too small for the expanding company. It ceased to build locomotives in 1871 when locomotive work transferred to Darlington North Road Works to allow the buildings to be utilised for wagon building.

15. Remote railway centres such as Shildon shed had to do quite heavy maintenance. On the hoist is NER 0-8-0 class T (LNER Q5) no. 792. Built at Gateshead in October 1903 it was withdrawn in November 1950. Over the years the facilities were expanded and improved. At its peak, the site covered some 40 acres of which 11 were under cover. It employed some 2,750 people. Its Railway Institute where workers could attend mutual improvement classes also opened in 1833 with Timothy Hackworth becoming its first President.

The works continued to build and repair wagons for the LNER and BR. In April 1982 British Rail Engineering Ltd (BREL) announced its intention to close the works, which at the time employed 2,600. Despite an extensive campaign to save it, the works closed its doors on 30th June 1984 with the completion of the last of 10,702 'Merry Go Round' hopper wagons built at Shildon. Hackworth Industrial Park was established on the site of the wagon works in 1985 using many of its former buildings. (R.Goad/ARPT)

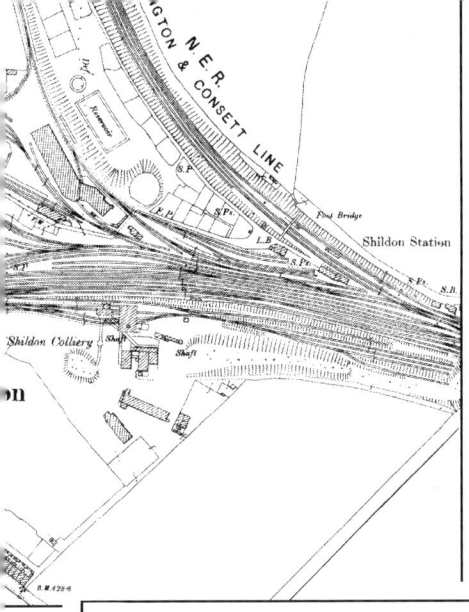

Shildon Locomotive Depot

Following the opening of the S&DR, Shildon became the HQ of the locomotive department and its engineering base and had shared facilities for both locomotives in operation and those undergoing major repairs. A new works was opened in 1833 to the west of the Masons Arms level crossing. To simplify matters a new nine-road straight shed was in use by 1849. A further building was built in 1852 for locomotive cleaning.

With the company expanding and more locomotives in traffic, it was not long before further accommodation was required. Three more sheds in long roundhouse form were added in 1854, 1856 and 1864, all three sheds having a central turntable which were connected through their central access road. A further building was added in 1873.

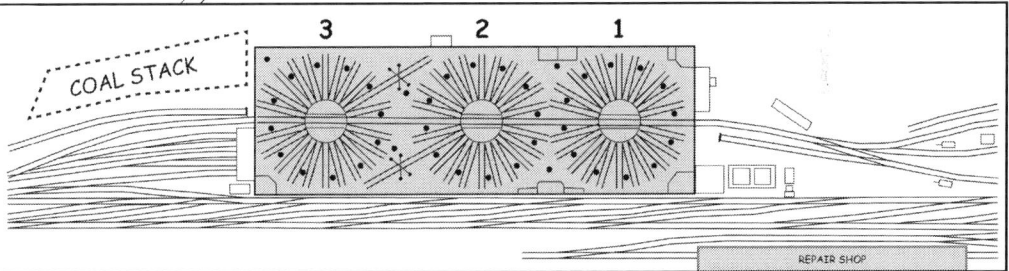

XII. The layout of the engine shed at Shildon drawn in its final form. No 1 turntable was on the right, no. 2 in the centre and the left hand one was no. 3. From 1886, rebuilding began which included the fitting of new turntables to no. 1 shed. All three turntables were completed by 1892.

Electrification resulted in no. 3 turntable being converted for exclusive use of the 10 electric locomotives that began working between Shildon and Newport (Middlesbrough) in 1915. All roads off no. 3 turntable were provided with overhead electrification wires. (Middleton Press)

Timetable extract from 1956 showing services between Darlington and Shildon, as well as services between Bishop Auckland and the now closed line to Tow Law.

16. Here are Bo-BoWE no. 5 (LNER 6492), no. 10 (LNER 6497), no. 3 (LNER 6490) and no. 7 (LNER 6494). The locomotives were used from Shildon to Newport on the Clarence Railway between 21st December 1914 and July 1935. The locomotives were later stored in Darlington Stooperdale paint shop and scrapped in 1950. When electrification was abandoned on 1st July 1935, it was decided to close Shildon shed and transfer locomotives and staff to West Auckland depot. The buildings after a period of disuse were adapted in 1937 for use as part of the wagon works and survive as part of the industrial park established on the site. (ARPT)

17. The central building is the hydraulic pump house for the Shildon wagon works in about 1923. It still stands today as part of the Hackworth Industrial Estate.
(Hackworth Victorian Museum/R.R.Darsley coll.)

18. This was the interior of the wagon works in 1913. Close examination shows both wooden and metal hopper wagons and one or two vans are present. (R.Goad/ARPT)

19. A visit to the BR wagon works in its last days when it was building steel hopper wagons for 'Merry Go Round' trains. The last wagon made here, HDA no. 368459, is in the Locomotion Railway Museum. (ARPT)

20. In the 1975 celebrations, locomotives were lined up for the Cavalcade. From left to right; GWR 0-6-0PT no. 7752, Caledonian Railway 0-4-4T no. 419, LMS 2MT 2-6-2T no. 41241, NER 0-8-0 no. 3395, 9F 2-10-0 no. 92220 *Evening Star*, LMS 4-6-0 no. 4767 *George Stephenson*, and NER 2-4-0 no. 910. (R.R.Darsley).

Masons Arms (Shildon)

XIII. The Masons Arms was adjacent to the level crossing which gave access to the works in later days. It is circled here in this 1946 map. The works yard was the assembly and stabling point for the 1975 Cavalcade.

Shildon would not be the last community to become a major railway centre, but it was without doubt the first – the world's first railway town. Opened with the line on 27th September 1825 the Masons Arms was not a station in the conventional sense as it had no other building nor platforms. The S&DR rented a room inside to act as a booking office and waiting room at a rent of £6 per annum. Passenger services could convey up to six people inside the coach and up to 20 outside (on the roof) and were licensed by the S&DR.

Initially, paper tickets for passenger services were written out by hand. Horse-drawn services remained until 1833 when passenger services came under S&DR control and were operated by steam locomotives. The current station site was developed and opened in 1842. This avoided the need for trains to reverse to access the line to Bishop Auckland through Shildon Tunnel.

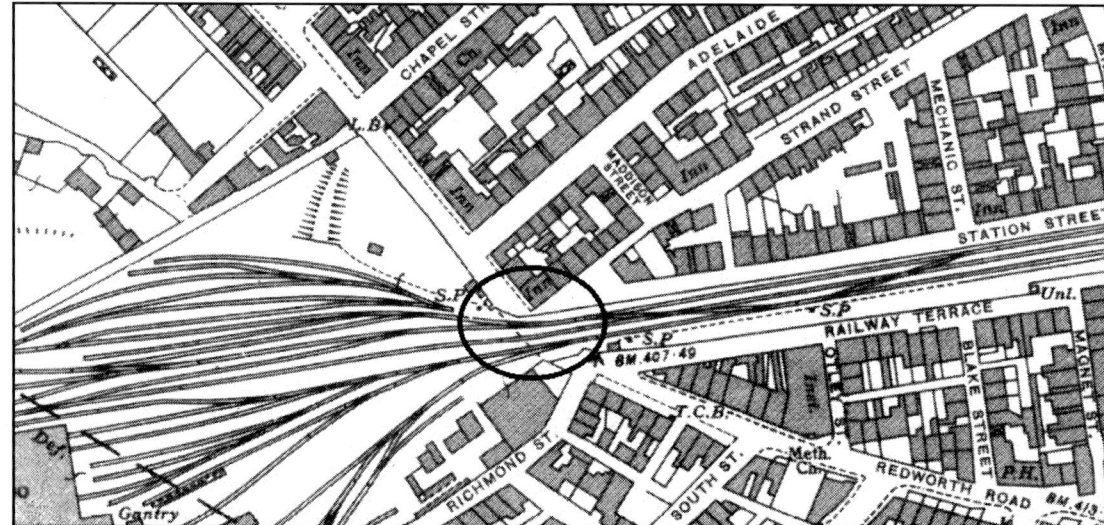

21. The wagon works was under the threat of closure on 21st September 1982 when class 08 diesel shunters 08268 and 08063 were at the entrance. Behind the locomotives is the Masons Arms used as an early station. It is now trading as 'Cape to Cairo'. (T.Heavyside)

Soho Works

XIV. The Soho Works of Timothy Hackworth as recorded in 1850. (Middleton Press)

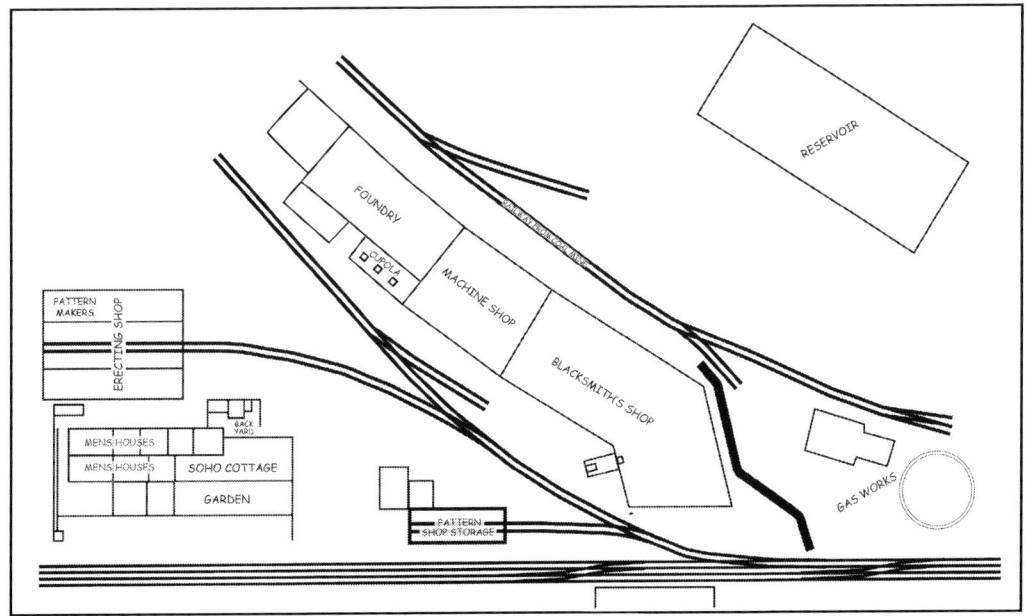

Hackworth entered his locomotive *Sans Pareil* in the Rainhill Trials in 1829. Although the locomotive suffered a breakdown, it was subsequently purchased by the Liverpool & Manchester Railway and later saw service with the Bolton & Leigh Railway before being withdrawn in 1844. After a spell as a colliery stationary boiler, it was acquired by the Science Museum and is now on display at Locomotion, Shildon. Hackworth died in July 1850 and the works ceased operations.

The surviving Soho building (now known as the Soho Shed) had been built in 1826 initially as a warehouse for an iron merchant. Fitted with underfloor heating, it was used as the locomotive paint shop during the 1870s. The building was then used for a variety of roles including a practise room for the works band before being taken out of use. After several years standing empty and threatened with demolition, it was restored as part of the Hackworth Museum following restoration in 1975. It subsequently became part of Locomotion, Shildon and was restored again in 2020. The Soho Works was purchased from the family in 1855 and used as an annexe to a new facility built west of the Masons Arms in 1833. All locomotive work was transferred to Darlington in 1883.

Prior to the opening of the S&DR, the 1821 population of Shildon was 115. It was Shildon that would become the engineering base of the new company on a green field site, which was soon known as New Shildon. Such towns would be established by railway companies around large workshops and other facilities the length and breadth of the country.

In 1831 Timothy Hackworth, who had been recruited by George Stephenson to join the S&DR in 1824, supervised the construction of the Soho Works, which was close to the house he lived in from 1831 (now a museum and part of the Locomotion complex). Hackworth became Locomotive Superintendent in 1825 and it was his determination in the following years that ensured that steam traction was developed and improved.

Hackworth had been born in Wylam in 1786 and was five years younger than George Stephenson who worked at the same colliery where Hackworth had served his apprenticeship as a blacksmith. By 1824 Hackworth was working for Robert Stephenson & Co in Newcastle and was involved in the construction of *Locomotion* and this resulted in his appointment and move to Shildon.

Soho Works was considered too small for the growing workload, which saw a move to new facilities. Hackworth negotiated to take over the original Soho works himself in partnership with Nicholas Downing and set up an independent engineering business, with Hackworth continuing in the employment of the S&DR whilst Thomas his brother looked after Hackworth's interests. The partnership was dissolved in 1837 when Hackworth became the sole owner. The works built locomotives for other lines, including those being developed overseas including one for Russia and another for Canada. Between 1839 and 1850 some 50 locomotives were constructed.

Shildon Coal Stage

22. Opened in 1873, it stood south of the main line to Witton Park and was located opposite Soho Works. The associated Shildon colliery closed on 15th March 1924. It was finally abandoned in February 1927.

The coal stage was built in 1847 and was the first attempt to mechanise coal loading for locomotives. It is seen here in use in 1933 but closed in 1935. The simple overhead catenary masts can also be seen, which were used by the electric locomotives between Shildon and Newport. Some of the local passenger services were then provided by Sentinel two-cylinder steam rail cars. Arriving in 1928, Shildon's allocation was *Neptune, Hero, Liberty, North Star* and from Selby in 1930, *True Blue*. When Shildon shed closed, the railcars were dispersed. This is thought to be *Liberty* coaling at the stage. The station and colliery can be seen on map XI, above picture 15.
(J.W.Armstrong/ARPT)

SHILDON

Shildon station was relocated to its current position in 1842 allowing closure of the short-lived facility alongside the Masons Arms. This simplified the operation of passenger trains which no longer needed to reverse to reach the Bishop Auckland line. The former railway sidings, Soho Works, and the goods yard (on map XI) is now part of the Locomotion complex and has undergone extensive restoration in recent years.

The station is currently served by Northern Trains between Saltburn and Bishop Auckland via Darlington and is marketed as the Bishop Line.

23. No. 4767 4-6-0 *George Stephenson* is a unique 'Black 5', in that it has Stephenson link motion. On 26th August 1975 it was working the shuttle service within the yards for the 1975 celebrations. GWR 0-6-0 pannier tank no.7752 was on the other end of the train. Behind the train are the coal drops and to the right are the tracks and down platform of the station. (G.W.Morrison)

24. A pre-grouping photograph of Shildon station with NER class R1 4-4-0 (later class D21) no.1240 on a Darlington train. Built in March 1909, the loco survived to May 1944. (Lens of Sutton Association/LOSA)

25. Shildon station with class B16/3 4-6-0 no. 61444 on a freight towards Bishop Auckland. This mixed traffic class, NER class S3, was the most successful of Raven's 4-6-0s. (K.Hoole coll./A.E.Young coll.)

➔ The ticket issued to one of the authors for the Grandstand to view the 1975 Calvacade.

26. An eight-car DMU, formed from four class 101 twin units, arrives at Shildon station for the S&DR 150th Anniversary locomotive cavalcade on 31st August 1975. These DMUs were built by Metropolitan-Cammell from 1956 and were one of the most successful first generation DMU. (T.Owen/Colour-Rail.com)

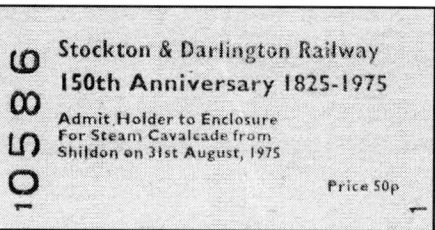

27. 'Pacer' class 143 no. 143025 is on a northbound train in June 1988. Built with Alexander bodies on Barclay frames the class were introduced in 1985 and withdrawn in 2022. The entrance track to the wagon works was disconnected after the works closed in 1984. (Colour-Rail.com.)

Shildon Yard (Thickley Sidings)

XV Shildon Yard in 1896. A colliery tramway comes down to Eden Pit from Middridge Colliery. The area towards the left-hand side, the Down yard, is now home to Locomotion Museum.

Shildon 'Laden Yard' opened in 1869 and was located on the up (north side) for loaded wagons. A smaller yard for empty wagons was on the down (south side) opened by the mid-1870s. It was closed as a major marshalling yard on 7th January 1935 though later it was part used for wagon storage awaiting repair at Shildon Works. Its fortunes revived during WWII when it handled greatly increased wartime traffic, providing relief to yards in the Darlington and Newcastle areas, trains being diverted away from the busy ECML to run via Shildon and Bishop Auckland. Thereafter, the relentless decline in freight resumed, with the up yard closed and all tracks lifted by the mid-1970s. However, the down yard survived until 1984 to handle wagons for Shildon works, which closed that year. The tracks were lifted by 1986 and part of the site used for the Locomotion Museum (see separate entry).

For the 1975 S&DR 150 Anniversary celebrations, it was on the site of the up yard that the grandstands were built for some 400,000 visitors to watch the procession of locomotives that had assembled at Shildon Works to join the line to Darlington on Sunday, 31st August that year (see photo 20) As a number of people pointed out at the time, by using the up yard site, the organisers had the photographers looking into the sun!

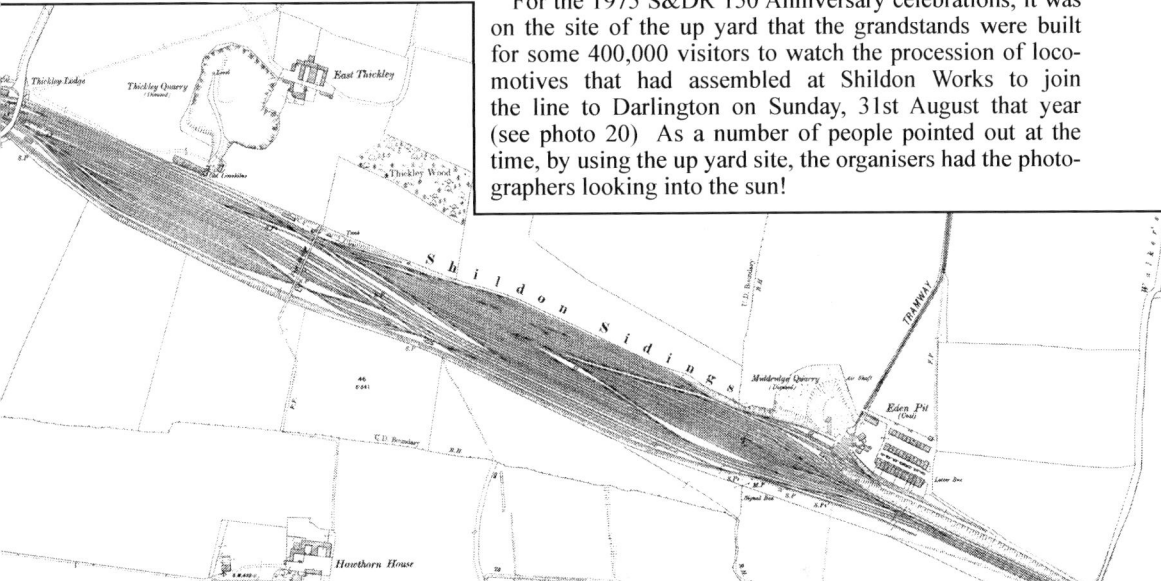

28. This is an early view of Thickley sidings taken from Salters Lane bridge. An NER tank engine is on a short freight train passing Eden Pit and the surviving S&DR overbridge is visible in the background. During the 1975 celebrations, commentary on the Cavalcade was given from this viewpoint. (E.Porteau/R.Humm coll.)

29. Thickley sidings on 2nd September 1964 has Fowler 4MT 2-6-4T no. 42405 hauling one passenger guards' van. This was the 3.48pm Darlington to Crook parcels, which became a passenger train on Fridays from Heighington to Crook, with one coach for workers from the Newton Aycliffe industrial estate. One 03 class 0-6-0DM and two class 24 Bo-BoDE with brake tenders are in the locomotive stabling sidings in the up yard. The S&DR bridge is in the background. The sidings on the right became the site of Locomotion, the National Railway Museum at Shildon. (R.Goad/ARPT)

Locomotion Museum, Shildon

30. The Collections Building for Locomotion Shildon, seen on 19th November 2018, was originally intended to be a storage shed but with the idea of opening for visitors on set days. The museum surprised everyone by having 94,000 visitors in the first six months after its opening on 12th October 2004. A second exhibition building was built in 2023. During the 1990s, the National Railway Museum's collection of locomotives, rolling stock and artefacts was unable to be accommodated in its entirety at the museum in York. Some were loaned out to the heritage railway sector or to other museums. Realising that the situation needed to be improved, the NRM, which is part of the Science Museum Group, set out to find another location that could house a second museum. This could accommodate and display up to 60 restored and part-restored vehicles from the national collection to be put on public display and was expected to attract 50,000 visitors annually. After looking at many sites, the railway town of Shildon provided the ideal location, with a brown-field site being located next to the former S&DR. Part of the site was already in use as the Hackworth Museum and the two were brought together in a joint-partnership between Durham County Council and the Science Museum Group. On 13th March 2002, the Heritage Lottery Fund announced a £4.9m grant towards the envisaged £7.7m cost of the new facility, enabling construction to proceed. The Durham County Council/Science Museum Group arrangement remained in place until 2017 when it became a fully owned subsidiary of the Science Museum Group.

Located on part of the old Shildon Down sidings area, the building would be linked to the former Timothy Hackworth Museum site by a ¼-mile rail shuttle. Initially known as the 'Shildon Railway Village', the more popular 'Locomotion – The National Railway Museum at Shildon' name was formally adopted in February 2004. Construction of the rail-served main display building commenced on 28th July 2003, with a first sod-cutting ceremony by the then local MP, the late Derek Foster, on 8th September 2003. Tracklaying at the new building was finished on 18th February 2004, whilst the main structure and roof had been completed. NER class T3 no. 901 was the first exhibit to arrive, on 16th June that year. Opening to the public on 27th September 2004 coincided with the day on which *Locomotion* hauled the first train out of Shildon to Stockton 179 years earlier.

The official opening took place on 22nd October 2004 when LMSR 'Coronation Pacific' no. 6233 *Duchess of Sutherland* hauled a special train to Shildon with guests including local Sedgefield MP and then Prime Minister, Tony Blair. The intended engine, LNER A3 'Pacific' no. 4472 *Flying Scotsman* had been declared a failure some weeks previously but was moved to Shildon in time for the opening ceremony.

Set a target of attracting 60,000 visitors in its first year, it saw 140,000 through the doors. It now averages around 200,000 per year and in January 2018 passed the 2.5m mark. (D.A.Lovett)

XVI. Site diagram of Locomotion showing the new building added in 2023. With the lead up to the bi-centenary in 2025, work started in 2020 to restore the historic buildings at the far end of the site next to Hackworth's house. Work commenced in 2023 on the construction of a second exhibition hall, which will house many more exhibits from the National Collection, doubling the covered exhibition space available. (National Railway Museum).

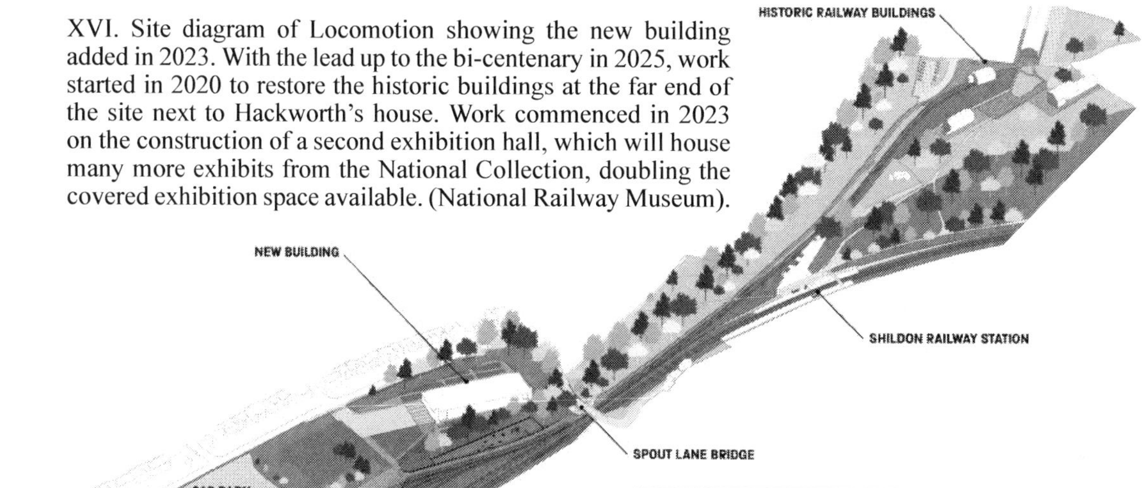

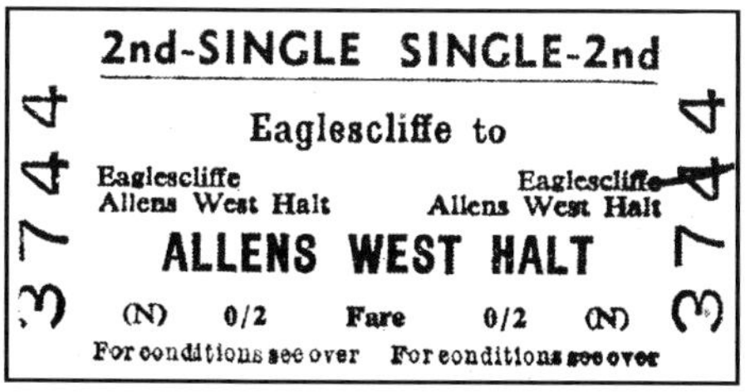

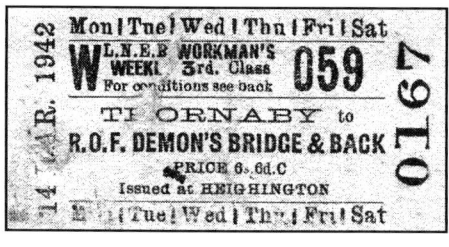

31. NER class D17/1 4-4-0 no. 1621 was outside Locomotion on 3rd November 2020. It was preserved because of its part in the 'Race to the North' in the summer of 1895. Behind is the LNER dynamometer car that records speed and power output. (D.A.Lovett)

32. Class A4 4-6-2 no. 4468 *Mallard* was in the museum on 7th November 2010. The streamlining development was part of the railways' quest for speed in the 1930s. The record registered for *Mallard* was 126mph, which was faster than the 125mph the Germans claimed for their 4-6-4 class 05 002 streamliner. (D.A.Lovett)

33. Relatively modern locomotives? The experimental gas turbine powered APT-E tilting train, the prototype DP1 'Deltic' whose two engines had a Napier triangular cylinder layout and the prototype High Speed Train (HSDT) Bo-BoDE class 41 no. 41001, all over 40 years old! They are seen here on 3rd November 2020. (D.A.Lovett)

34. 0-4-0ST Andrew Barclay no. 2361 of 1954 was named *W.S.T.* after a director's initials (William Stuart Trimble, former owner of the Long Meg Plaster & Mineral Co.) and here is running the Locomotion shuttle in the museum yard on 2nd December 2004. It was on loan from the Bowes Railway, Gateshead, which is the last place a rope incline railway can now be seen. (R.R.Darsley)

3. Shildon to North Road

Simpasture Junction (Clarence Railway to Port Clarence)

This was the junction for the former Clarence Railway, originally promoted as the Tees & Weardale Railway before changing its name to the Clarence Railway in 1826, as it was not going anywhere close to Weardale. It was opened in August 1833 from its junction with the S&DR at Simpasture to Haverton Hill near Stockton on the River Tees. It was subsequently extended to Port Clarence in 1834. The railway took its name from the Duke of Clarence, who later became King William IV whose reign lasted from 1830 until his death in 1837.

The railway seemed to be built by the faction who supported the canal or a more direct rail route to Stockton. It could not, however, penetrate the coal field around Shildon itself and had to rely on its rival the S&DR to transport the coal from the pits to the junction. At first it was highly successful and extracted considerable traffic away from the S&DR. This presented a problem for the S&DR, who could either starve the Clarence of traffic or charge it handsomely for the privilege. Not surprisingly the Clarence was soon in financial difficulty and was the subject of early mergers.

The Clarence was leased to the Stockton & Hartlepool Railway in August 1844. In June 1852, the Stockton & Hartlepool merged with the Hartlepool & West Harbour & Dock Company and purchased the Clarence Railway. They became part of the NER in 1865. It was only after both the Clarence and S&DR were under NER ownership that both routes became viable, the Clarence subsequently becoming the electrified line from Shildon to Newport Yard (now Tees Yard) near Middlesbrough.

XVII. The junction with the Clarence Railway is seen in this 6ins to 1 mile map of 1898. The Clarence route only ever saw short-lived passenger services on the section from Simpasture Junction and Stillington North Junction. From 11th July 1835 it carried a Clarence Railway service from Stockton to Shildon, believed to be intermittent, operating until 12th February 1842. On the same date, an S&DR service between Darlington (North Road) and Coxhoe (near Ferryhill), which involved reversals at both Simpasture Junction and Stillington North Junctions, also ceased after having only been introduced on 30th November 1841. Finally, workers' services operated during WWII in connection with the Royal Ordnance Factory at Aycliffe (see overleaf). Apart from railtours and the annual Bishop Auckland to Seaton Carew Sunday excursions, the line was not used. Simpasture Junction to Stillington North Junction finally closed on 24th June 1963.

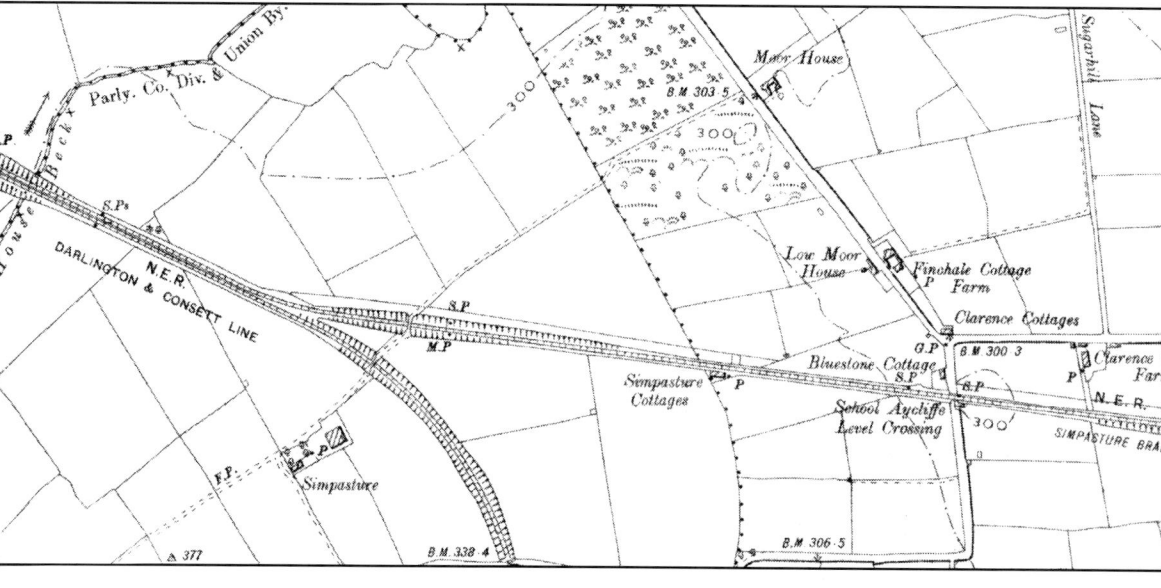

35. NER Bo-BoWE no. 4 is on a train on the Clarence Railway heading towards Simpasture Junction in August 1923. The Clarence Railway was built in competition to the S&DR with its coal drops on the north bank of the Tees. (Photomatic/R.Humm)

NEWTON AYCLIFFE

XVIII. The station at Newton Aycliffe is adjacent to a golf complex. The post-war New Towns Act of 1946 created the new town of Newton Aycliffe, planning of which began in 1947. West and south of this site was the old town quarry sidings. A station had been envisaged to serve the town from the outset, located in the 'V' of Simpasture Junction with platforms on both the S&DR and Clarence routes. In the event various factors delayed its provision by many years, well beyond closure of the latter line, so by the time Newton Aycliffe station opened on 9th January 1978, on the site of Simpasture Junction, it had platforms on the S&DR route only. It is still in use today by Bishop Line services. (Middleton Press)

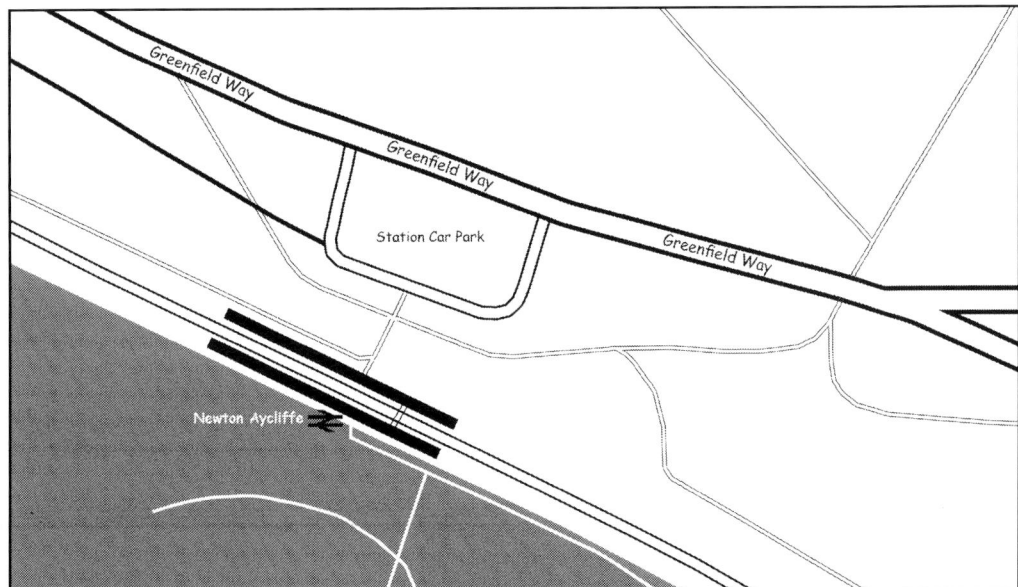

36. The station for the new town was opened by British Railways on 9th January 1978. This photograph, looking west, was taken on 17th August 1978, seven months later. (A.E.Young)

Royal Ordnance Factory, Aycliffe

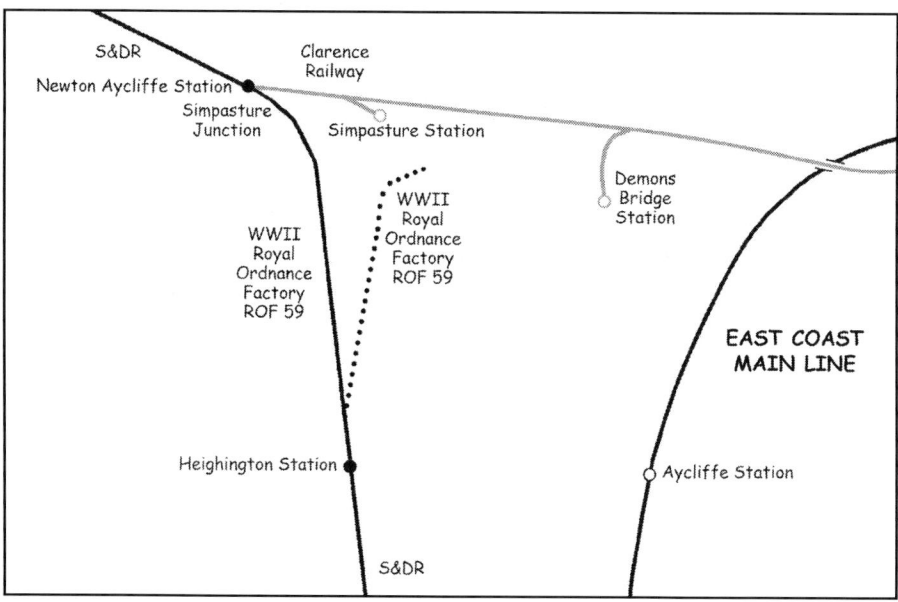

XIX.   Diagram showing the two wartime stations at Simpasture and Demons Bridge (on the Clarence Railway). Both served the The Royal Ordnance Factory Aycliffe, built in 1940 and opened in April 1941. The site was also served by a third station, Heighington, on the S&DR. ROF Aycliffe was built on both sides of the S&DR route, between Simpasture Junction and Heighington and was bounded by the former Clarence Railway route from Simpasture Junction on the northern side.

The site was chosen because it stood on marsh land and for much of the year was covered in fog or mist and therefore not easily identifiable to passing Luftwaffe pilots. Such sites were deliberately located away from conurbations just in case a major accident occurred! Although there were many minor ones which resulted in loss of life, there was no loss of production.

Covering 867 acres it opened for production of bullets, shells and mines in 1941. It employed some 17,000 people working three shifts, seven days a week, 90% of them women. They were known as 'Aycliffe Angels', named in a broadcast from Germany by Nazi propagandist 'Lord Haw Haw' (William

Joyce). Many of these were transported to the site by train from surrounding towns. The work was dangerous. Eight employees were killed in an explosion on the day before VE day in 1945.

The Prime Minister Winston Churchill visited the site in May 1942. It is known that several radio personalities visited such as Gracie Fields and Wilfred Pickles who entertained the staff there.

To cope with the demand, Heighington station was extended, and additional shelters built. This station was used mainly by special trains operating from Darlington and Saltburn. Other services operated to new stations at Demons Bridge (opened 14th December 1941) and Simpasture (opened 18th January 1942) both served by short branch lines off the former Clarence Railway. Simpasture had four terminal platforms and was served by trains from Bishop Auckland, Tow Law, Durham and the Wear Valley. Six terminal platforms were provided at Demons Bridge to cater for workers being brought in from Hartlepool, Seaham and Teesside. The ROF's extensive internal rail system was operated by seven new steam and one diesel 0-4-0 locomotives, delivered during 1941-43. The ROF closed in September 1945 and workers' trains ceased to both Demons Bridge and Simpasture termini by 1st October, WWII had ended in Europe on 7th May 1945 and in Japan on 2nd September 1945, thus rendering the facility redundant.

XX. The 1953 map of the former ROF facility shows that the industrial estate was rail-served at that time. The buildings went on to form the Aycliffe Industrial Estate, established in October 1945 and operated by North Eastern Trading Estates Ltd, providing employment for the New Town of Newton Aycliffe, which was an early post-war development, many ex-ROF employees providing a ready workforce. Heighington station served the needs of workers travelling by rail to the new estate. Two of the former ROF steam engines and a newly acquired diesel locomotive worked the trading estate railway system until 1961 when shunting was taken over by BR. Siding connections into the estate survived until the 1960s, controlled from Heighington signal box. The Industrial Estate still thrives with many of the buildings being replaced by more modern structures.

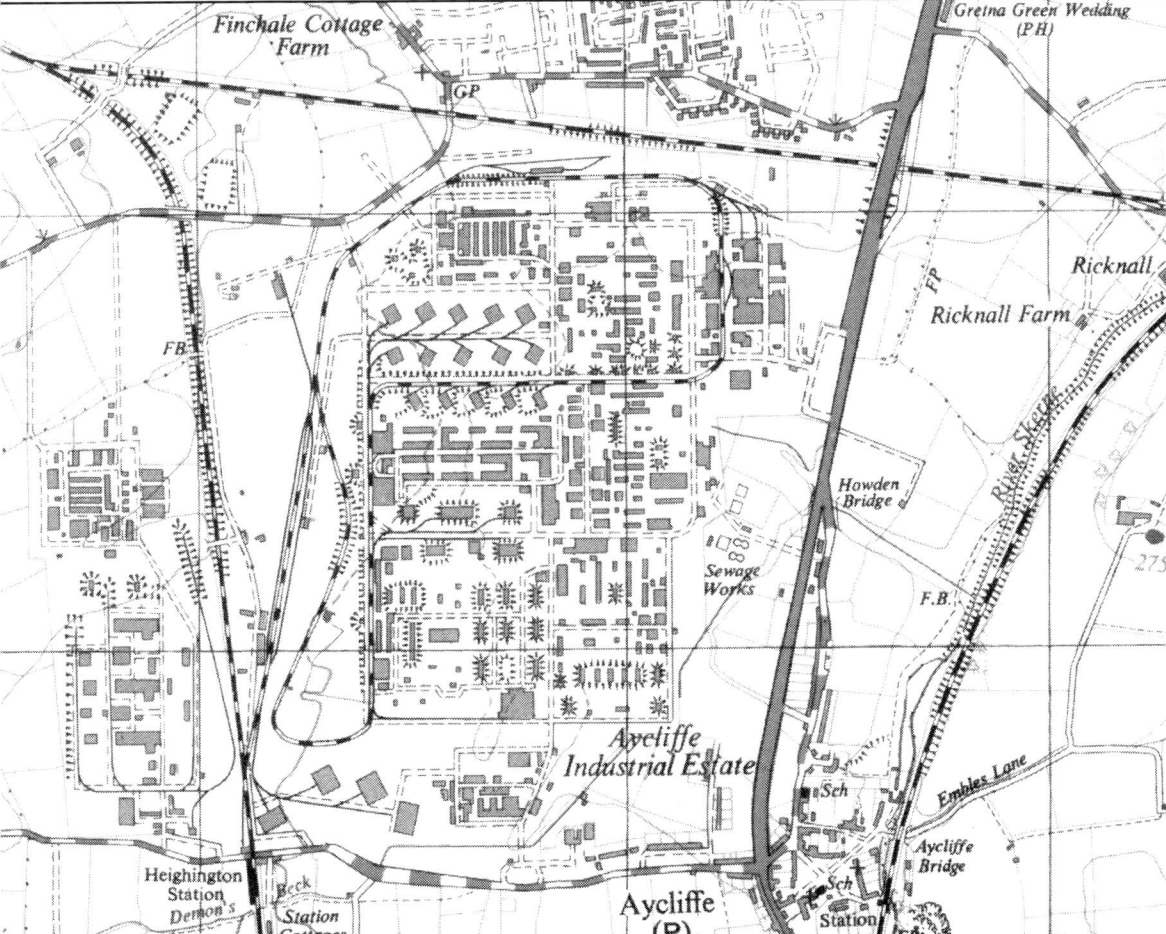

37. This was Newton Aycliffe station on 11th December 2018. As part of the Tees Valley Metro project the station was given new shelters and an information system. There is currently an hourly service. (D.A.Lovett)

38. Newton Aycliffe station on the same day but facing eastwards. There was another station, Aycliffe, situated on the East Coast mainline which closed on 2nd March 1953. This features in our albums *Darlington to Newcastle* and *Darlington-Leamside-Newcastle*. (D.A.Lovett)

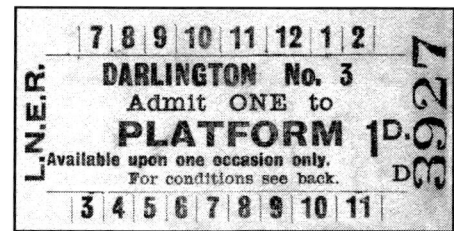

HEIGHINGTON

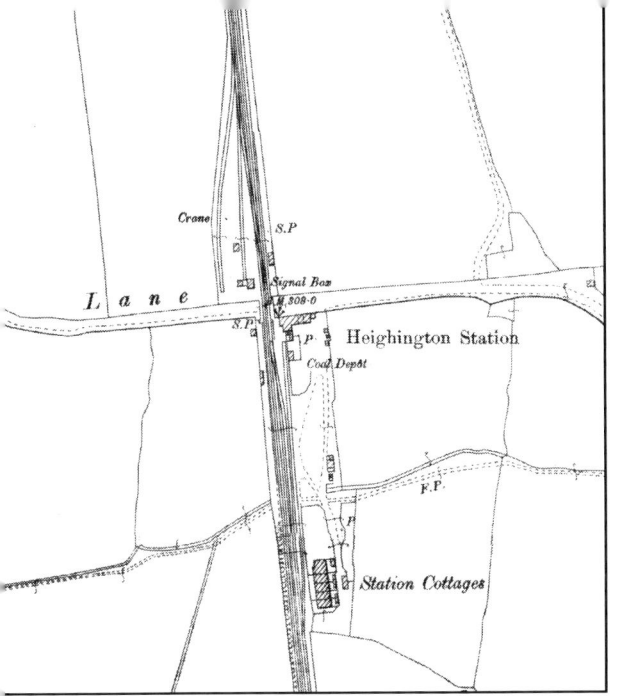

XXI. The station is seen here in 1897. Originally opened as Aycliffe Lane in 1826, it was subsequently named Aycliffe & Heighington before becoming Aycliffe on 1st July 1871. It was renamed Heighington on 1st September 1874. By 1840 the crossing keeper was able to issue tickets.

It was here on 1st July 1828 that the boiler of *Locomotion* exploded, killing the driver. Ironically, it had been delivered here from Stephenson's Works in Newcastle. It was placed on the rails in September 1825.

Improvements were made during WWII to provide additional accommodation for the adjacent Royal Ordnance Factory. This included the provision of longer platforms and additional shelters. The station lost its goods facilities on 2nd March 1970.

39. A general view of Heighington showing the signal box and level crossing built in 1872. The S&DR station building, of about 1827, and the later NER signal box are both Grade II listed. (R.Humm coll.)

40. The public houses were the original places to purchase tickets. Four pubs, at Heighington, Darlington, Yarm and Stockton, were built and owned by the S&DR, Here is the mural of *Locomotion* on the back of the pub wall at Heighington on 7th April 2015; more recently the pub has appeared closed. (R.R.Darsley)

41. During World War II long canopies were built on the platforms as shelter for the commuting ordnance workers. The view is towards Darlington. (R.Humm coll.)

42. A class K1 2-6-0, possibly no. 62004 or 62064, on a northbound freight goes through the station. This was a Peppercorn class introduced in 1949. The goods yard, which closed on 2nd March 1970, is on the right. Most of the war time ROF freight came out via Heighington. (R.Humm coll.)

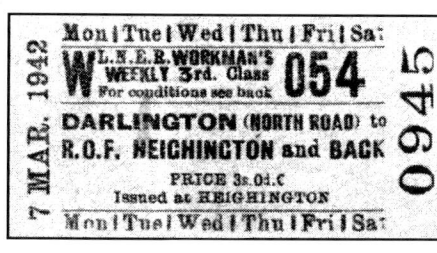

43. Class 156 DMU no. 156479 goes south on 11th December 2015. The 156 class are Metro-Cammell Super Sprinters, second generation DMUs introduced in 1988. The station area has now been minimised to the two platforms and 'bus' shelters. (D.A.Lovett)

44. This is the present station and level crossing. If you look close to the passenger shelter, you will see that the platform has a 'Harrington Hump', a small, raised platform to avoid the need for steps or raising the whole platform length, named after the first station where it was piloted, Harrington in Cumbria. (R.R.Darsley)

Hitachi Rail Europe Newton Aycliffe (Merchant Park)

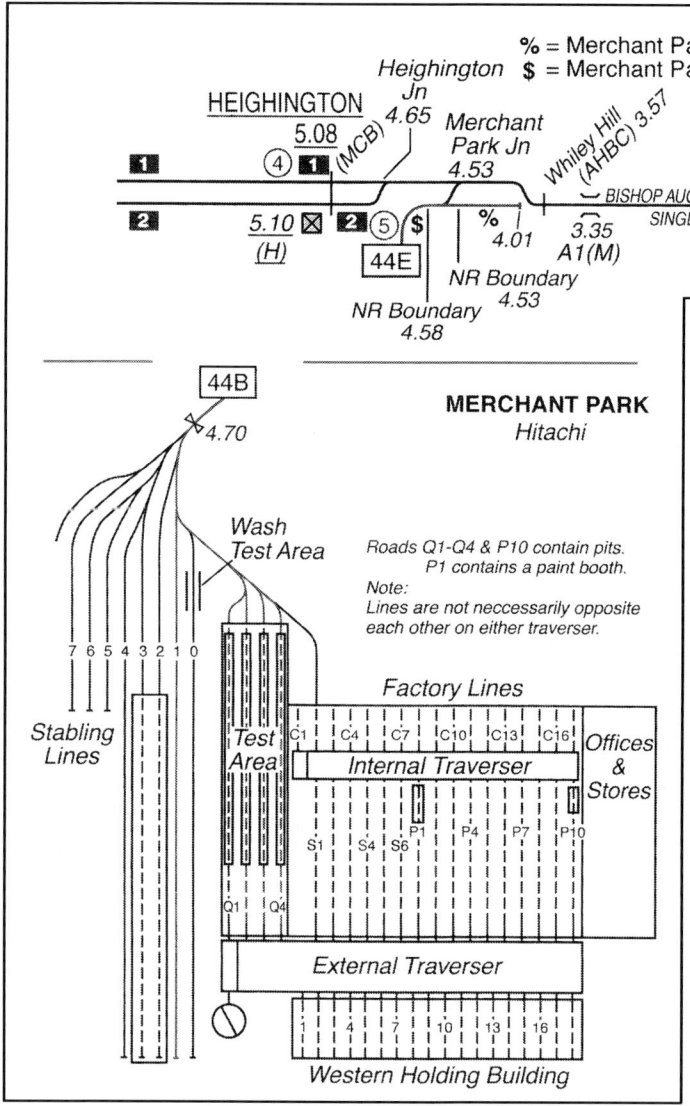

XXII. Diagrams of the track layout at Hitachi's Newton Aycliffe facility.

This new factory was formally opened on 3rd September 2015 by then Prime Minister David Cameron and covers 31.5 acres covering 475,000ft². Construction commenced in November 2013. Built at a cost of £100m, it employs some 700 people and can build 10 carriages a week when operating at capacity. It is linked to the Bishop Auckland line by a short branch line commissioned on 25th March 2015 with a 25kV electrified test track running parallel to the Down line.

By 2021 the factory had completed large orders of Intercity Express Programme (IEP) classes 800/801 electric and bi-mode high-speed trains for both Great Western Railway and LNER, together with a small fleet of 5 class 803 electric IEPs for First Group 'Lumo' ECML services. It also built class 385 EMUs for ScotRail and is building the bodyshells for the 54 new eight car trains for HS2 (the new High-Speed line between Euston, Birmingham, Manchester and the East Midlands) in partnership with Alstom at Crewe and Derby. (©TRACKmaps)

45. The IEP Merchant Park Sidings were devised to give both a works entrance and an electrified test line of 1½km. The fence and the OHL were not yet completed on 7th April 2015. The site was officially opened on 3rd September 2015. (R.R.Darsley)

46. An aerial photograph of the Hitachi manufacturing facility shows class 385 and early class 800 sets in the sidings. Top soil and drainage excavation formed the lake and nature reserve to the north of the factory. (Hitachi Rail Europe Ltd)

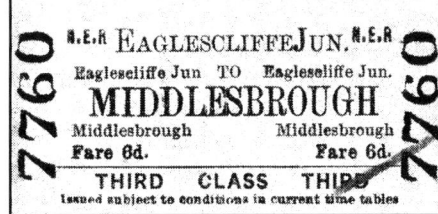

47. On 21st June 2018 two of the Hitachi shunters are in the sidings with new class 385. The shunters are class 08 0-6-0DE no. 08484 *Captain Nathaniel Darell* belonging to Railway Support Services Ltd, and Zephyr road/rail 4wDH 2631 of 2016. (R.R.Darsley)

48. LNER 'Azuma' class 800 units were seen under inspection in the yards on 13th April 2017. 'Azuma' means 'East' and they are part of the Hitachi AT300 family. The bi-modal (diesel and electric) units came in nine car (800/1) and five car (800/2) units. In the early days they suffered from fatigue cracking in the area of the yaw dampers. (R.R.Darsley)

Charity Junction / Hopetown Junction / Stooperdale Junction

XXIII. The triangular junction dominates this 6ins map dated 1952. Whessoe Works was also accessed off the line (see following entry) A triangular junction was accessed from the north at Charity Junction and from the south at Hopetown Junction with both lines converging at Stooperdale Junction to the west. The impressive Faverdale Wagon Works is in the middle of the map.

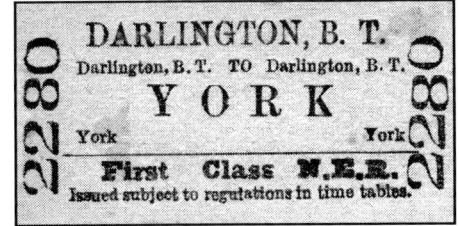

49. Charity Junction signal box, seen in 1965, was northwest of North Road station and controlled the junction with the Barnard Castle line from the Shildon direction and also the entrance to West Works and Rise Carr sidings.

Promoted as the Darlington & Barnard Castle Railway, Hopetown Junction is where the Barnard Castle line diverged, opening on 8th July 1856. It was later extended to Tebay and Penrith over Stainmore. Barnard Castle became the junction for lines to Middleton-in-Teesdale and Bishop Auckland. Passenger services between Darlington and Middleton-in-Teesdale were withdrawn on 30th November 1964 with goods traffic ceasing on 5th April 1965. The rails were removed soon after.

The junctions also provided access to the Stooperdale works and the nearby Faverdale Wagon Works, which was opened in August 1923 when its first wagons were built. It became a wagon repair centre in 1959, with new wagon builds taking place at nearby Shildon. The wagon works at Faverdale closed in June 1963. (D.Butterfield/R.Humm coll.)

50. LNER class J39 0-6-0 no. 1425 passes through Faverdale. Built at Darlington in December 1929 and renumbered in BR days as no. 64813, this was a local locomotive until withdrawal at the end of 1962. (J.W.Armstrong/ARPT)

Faverdale Wagon Works

51. Faverdale had a wagon works and this is the interior about 1930 with sign-writers hand-painting six plank wagons. The works could, it was said, turn out 200 wagons a week.
(Sport & General/ R.Humm coll.)

52. In 1925, the centenary of the S&DR was celebrated with a display of locomotives at Faverdale. Here is NER long boilered 0-6-0 no. 1275 built by Dubs (707/1874) and which currently is at the Railway Museum, York.
(J.W.Armstrong/ ARPT)

Whessoe Works

The company owned by W & A Kitching began operating a foundry as part of its ironmonger's business in 1790. It secured contracts from the S&DR, its owners being financial supporters of the scheme and William becoming a director of the railway company until his death in 1850.

In 1831 they moved to a new site at Hopetown adjacent to the S&DR. It was here that several locomotives were built including the Hackworth designed *Derwent* in 1845 which survived and is now part of the National Collection. It has been on display at the North Road Station Museum (formerly Head of Steam) since 1975. It was presented to the NER for preservation in 1898 by its then colliery owners. It was displayed for some years at Darlington Bank Top on a plinth alongside *Locomotion*.

In 1860 the site was sold to the S&DR as part of the development in readiness for the opening of its own North Road works in 1863. The Whessoe Foundry business moved elsewhere in the town and continues in business servicing the oil and gas industry.

Whessoe Road Engine Shed (near North Road)

The four road Whessoe Road Engine Shed is a remarkable survivor It can be seen in map XXIV below, as can the later roundhouses.

An engine shed was established at North Road in early S&DR days. It served as a sub-shed of Shildon. It appears to have been small and could accommodate only two or three locomotives. Several attempts were made to improve the situation although it took until 1861 when a new facility was added in the form of a straight shed to accommodate 12 locomotives. To cope with demand, a roundhouse was added in 1868 and another in 1877 in the north yard of the Locomotive works, which had opened in 1863. The straight shed later became a paint shop

and finally a diesel test house. The two roundhouses were used until 1903 when locomotives were transferred to the enlarged depot near Bank Top. After 1903 the roundhouses were used for the works shunters and by locomotives awaiting works attention.

After closure and demolition of the works, the 1861 straight shed fell into disuse before being leased for industrial use. It remains in Network Rail ownership.

The shed is currently being restored and returned to railway use as part of the development of the Darlington Railway Heritage Quarter in readiness for the 2025 Anniversary.

Darlington North Road Loco Works

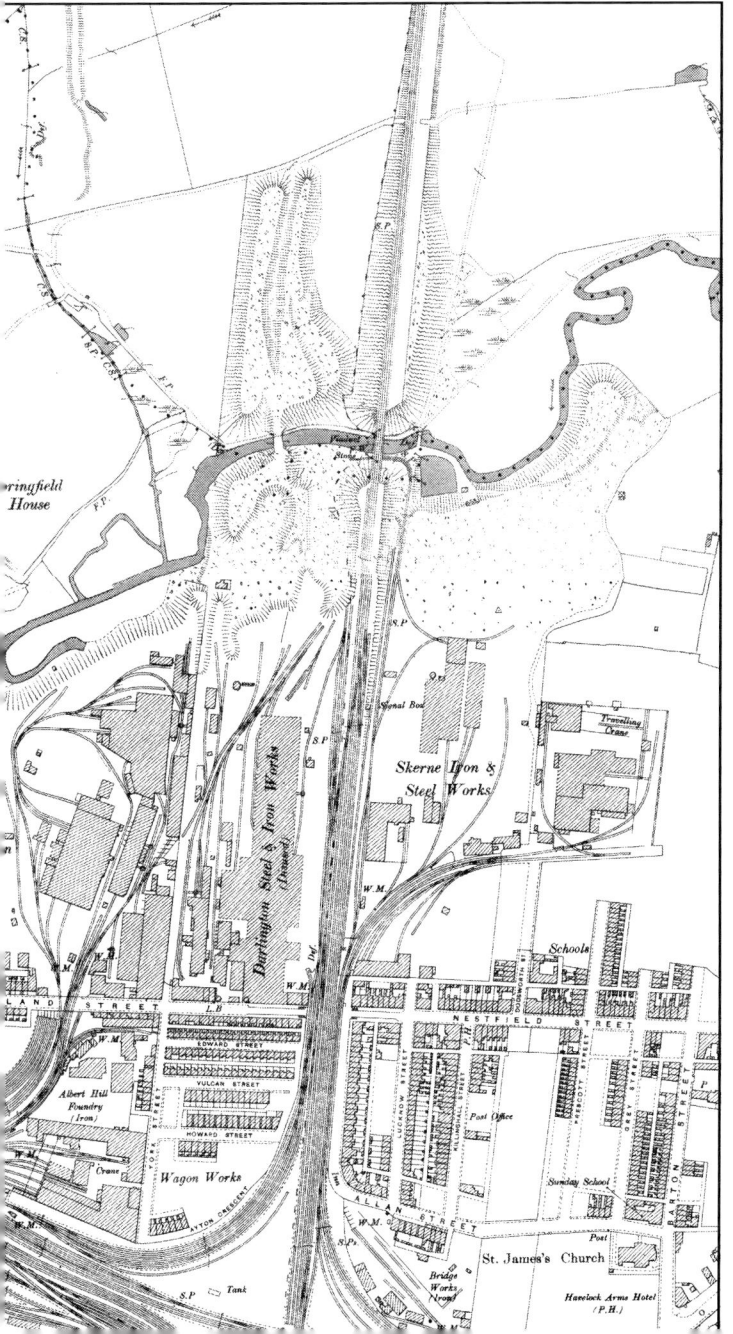

← XXIV. The North Road locomotive works in 1897 with the two roundhouses clearly seen. The rows of terraced houses around the works are similar to those found around major works to accommodate the workforce.

Opened in 1863 by the S&DR, the works passed into NER ownership later that year. It built the first NER designed locomotives in 1877, 14 years after the S&DR had amalgamated with the NER in 1863.

The works hosted an exhibition of locomotives in 1875 to celebrate the 50th Anniversary of the S&DR.

In 1911-12, major extensions to the works were built on the Stooperdale site, consisting of boiler, tender and paint shops, plus a fine new office building, designed by William Bell, opened in April 1912 for the NER Chief Mechanical Engineer. Sir Vincent Raven was the first to take up residence along with his staff, who had previously transferred from Gateshead to North Road in 1910.

The works closed on 1st April 1966. The site now houses a supermarket (Morrisons) and leisure facilities. The Stooperdale Office is Grade II listed and is currently the Rail Staff Pensions Office.

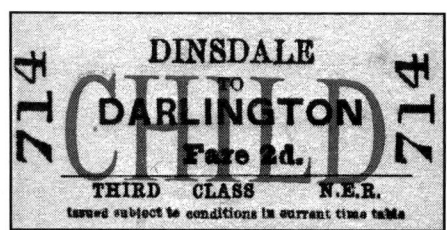

53. Darlington locomotive works on 24th March 1946 showing the main repair depot, the locomotive weigh houses and the tyre park. Of the locos visible only the ex-works ones are identifiable: class J26 0-6-0 no. 5742 and class A8 4-6-2T no. 9858. (LNER/R.Humm coll.)

54. The interior of the erecting shop with class J27 0-6-0 no. 65880, class K1 2-6-0 no. 62004 and 8F 2-8-0 no. 905xx. The date is 22nd March 1965. (P.J.Robinson)

55. One of the joys of Darlington was the monthly visits by the North East branch of the RCTS and others. It was always good to find 'foreigners' in corners of the works. In the line-up during September 1965 is LMS 8F 2-8-0 no. 48169.
(S.B.Lee/ Colour-Rail.com)

56. On 10th June 1951 the new steam build included Ivatt 2-6-0s. Darlington built both 38 of the LMS version in 1953 and the entire class of 65 of the very similar BR 78xxx from 1952.
(G.H.Hunt/ Colour-Rail.com)

57. When class A3 4-6-2 no. 4472 *Flying Scotsman* went into private preservation in January 1963, it was prepared at Doncaster Works. On 22nd March 1965 it came to Darlington Works for an overhaul and a change of boiler.
(R.R.Darsley coll.)

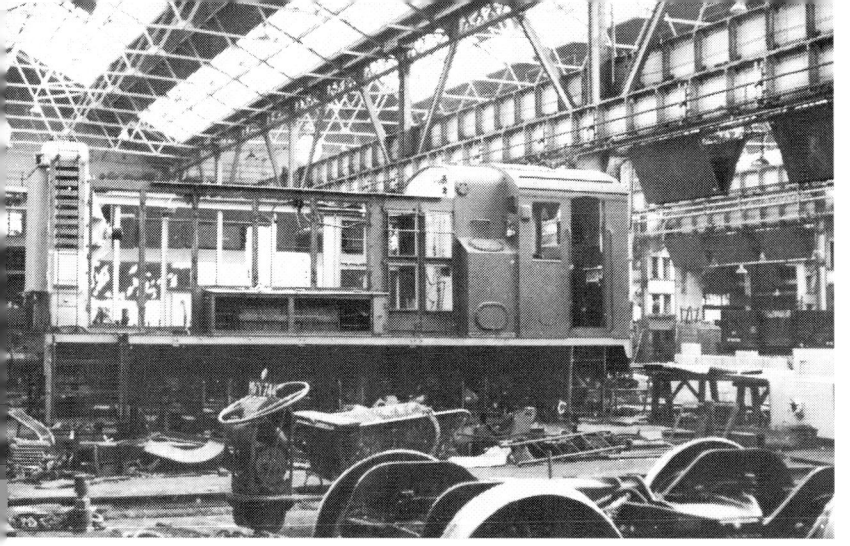

58. Darlington Works diesel construction and repair is typified by class 11 0-6-0DE no. 12117 stripped down on 22nd December 1965. A LMS precursor of the 08 class, all of the class had gone by November 1972 with a number sold on for industrial use.
(R.R.Darsley coll.)

↙ 59. The Diesel engine shop in Darlington loco works as it was on 24th August 1963.
(T.Owen/
Colour-Rail.com)

↓ 60. A melancholy but interesting area of the works was the scrapyard situated at North Road station. Here, in their final days, are 4-6-0 class B16 nos 61413 and 61443. The tank engine is class L1 2-6-4T no. 67750. This L1 was built by North British Locomotive Company in 1948 but their work was taken over by diesel multiple units. The year was 1962. (ARPT)

61. D20 class 4-4-0 nos 62375 and 62383 were two of six of the class that finished their days on Newcastle to Alnmouth trains. Though reported in the scrapyard in April 1955, no. 62383 was rescued from there for a further six months' work. Its NER tender had been scrapped already so it was replaced with a straight sided LNER version. It was finally withdrawn on 12th May 1957. (P.J.Robinson)

Darlington Depot branch

XXV. The Darlington Depot branch was opened with the line in 1825 to supply coal to the residents of Darlington through a depot at North Bridge half a mile away. It was nearer to the centre of town than the main facilities at North Road.

It was cut back in 1896 to the area around Hopetown Carriage Works and was used latterly for the cutting up of steam locomotives following withdrawal.

The short-lived facility near Northgate Bridge served as a coal depot. North Road station is in the centre of this 1858 map. The carriage works at Hopetown is clearly marked and continued in use after the Depot Branch was cut back and a coal depot established at North Gate.

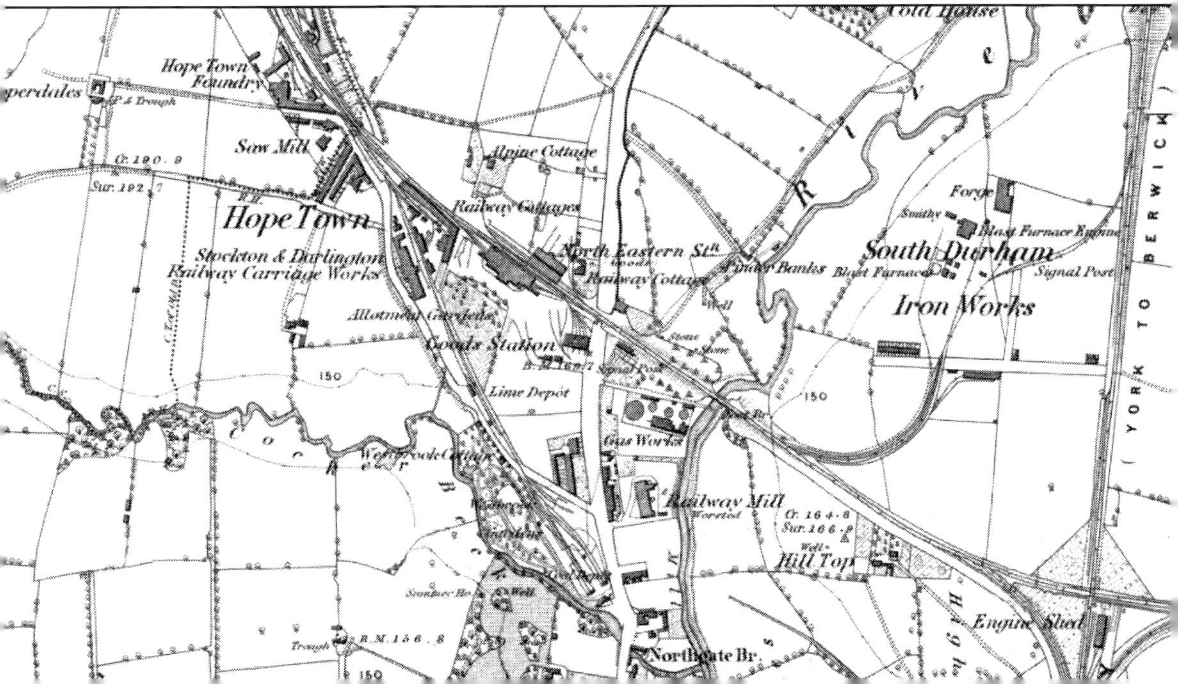

Hopetown Carriage Works

The carriage works was opened in 1853 to build and maintain two axle coaches. Designed by Joseph Spark it comprised a long two track shed divided by a two-storey central section, which contained lifting equipment. Access was by turntables. It was built alongside and accessed from the Darlington Depot branch.

The building continued in use until 1884 repairing coaches and wagons when coach construction was transferred to York Works and wagon construction concentrated at Shildon Works. It was later used as a store and a rifle range.

It was acquired by Darlington Borough Council during the 1980s and listed (Grade II) in 1986. It now forms part of Hopetown Darlington (formerly Head of Steam and Darlington Railway Centre and Museum) which is centred on the nearby Darlington North Road station.

In 1995 the council signed an agreement with the A1 Steam Locomotive Trust, who subsequently built a new LNER A1 class there, no. 60163 *Tornado*. The north wing is currently occupied by the North Eastern Locomotive Preservation Group (NELPG) who own several steam locomotives, most of which are in use on the North Yorkshire Moors Railway (NYMR). Locomotives undergoing major works are restored at the Darlington site whilst routine maintenance is carried out in the NELPG's facilities at Grosmont on the NYMR.

62. This is the exterior of the Hopetown carriage works on 11th April 1995. The 0-4-0DM Ruston Hornsby 312988/1952 was used together with the modified guards van to give shuttle rides for the Darlington Railway Preservation Society (DRPS). The coach was E51203, a class 101 power car which was unfortunately destroyed by vandals. (R.R.Darsley)

63. The interior of the carriage works, reborn as the Darlington Locomotive works, was where the replica class A1 4-6-2 no. 60163 *Tornado* was built, seen here on 24th September 2007. The next replica being built here is class P2 2-8-2 no. 2006 *Prince of Wales*. The building is due to become the Ken Hoole Study Centre in plans for the Railway Heritage Quarter. (R.R.Darsley)

NORTH ROAD (DARLINGTON)

North Road takes its name from being adjacent to the Great North Road, which linked London and Edinburgh during the stagecoach era, later becoming the A1. As passenger services were operated by contractors initially there were no stations with platforms. Public houses were used, 'The Talbot' fulfilling this role at North Road, with regular services commencing 10th October 1825. The road is now the A167 – the current day A1(M) by-passing to the west of Darlington since 1965.

Named Hopetown Goods, a three-storey goods station was provided between the current facility and the Skerne Bridge. When the S&DR took over passenger services in 1833, it became the first station. It appears in at least one early illustration to the side of an embankment with the top storey adjacent to the line. The goods station can also be seen in map XXIV.

A new temporary station to the west of what is now the current station was authorised in May 1840 and came into use soon after. A more permanent station was then under construction, designed by the S&DR's resident engineer John Harris, which opened in April 1842. It was not long, however before Bank Top became the main station; it benefitted from being nearer to the town centre. North Road's location on the northern edge of Darlington was less than ideal and once the NER controlled all the lines in the area, all passenger services were diverted through Bank Top station from 1st July 1887 and then took the new line towards Stockton at Darlington South Junction.

Over the years North Road has had several name variations. It was for a time known as Darlington but after the opening of Darlington Bank Top on 31st March 1841, the S&DR station became known as North Road or Hopetown. The decision was taken that the station would be known as North Road and the adjacent goods facilities Hopetown. By October 1868 it was appearing in timetables as Darlington North Road but by September 1934 it reverted to North Road.

North Road became a junction station with the opening of the line to Barnard Castle on 8th July 1856. This was subsequently extended over Stainmore to Kirkby Stephen where services split to Penrith in the north and Tebay. Services ran to and from Bank Top and from 13th May 1868 trains to Middleton-in-Teesdale also served North Road. North Road was threatened with closure as early as the 1930s but remained until threatened again by the Beeching Cuts outlined in 1963. Again, it survived due to the retention of the Bishop Auckland service.

In 1969, North Road was reduced to an unstaffed halt and from 1972 only the former up platform remained in use for Bishop Auckland services upon singling of the line to Heighington. The station buildings soon fell into disrepair and suffered vandalism. Concern for its future was expressed and in 1975 it was restored by Darlington Borough Council with most of the station becoming the North Road railway museum, formally reopened on 27th September that year by the late HRH Duke of Edinburgh on the exact S&DR 150th Anniversary. Subsequently, the site was renamed the Darlington Railway Centre & Museum and refurbishment took place with funding provided by the Heritage Lottery Fund. The site is on a 200-year lease from NR. From 2008 it was known as the Head of Steam railway museum. Between 2022-24 the museum and surrounding heritage buildings were transformed into a brand new visitor attraction, Hopetown Darlington.

64. A class 101 DMU is leaving North Road station heading for Shildon on 19th February 1983. In the background is the cleared site of the Hopetown Goods Yard and West Marshalling Yard used for westbound traffic towards Bishop Auckland. (Colour-Rail.com)

65. A rail tour was in North Road station on 4th September 1955. It was the Northern Dales tour organised by the Stephenson Locomotive Society and the Manchester Locomotive Society. It arrived at North Road from Tebay behind J21 class 0-6-0 no. 65061 and 2MT 2-6-0 no. 46478. A8 class 4-6-2T no. 69855 took the train from North Road to Eaglescliffe via the older 'Fighting Cocks' route. At Eaglescliffe no. 69855 ran round the train and took it on to Northallerton. (A.G.Ellis/R.Humm coll.)

66. The classic exterior of North Road station is seen on 23rd August 1976. It is currently the North Road Station Museum, housing the Ken Hoole Study Centre, and is part of Hopetown Darlington. (A.E.Young)

67. Inside the museum is the original 0-4-0 *Locomotion*. This was on 11th July 2011. The National Railway Museum has moved it to Shildon, which upset Darlington, as the locomotive appears on the town's crest and it spent many years displayed at Bank Top station. A compromise has been worked out in the preparations for the S&DR 200 years' celebration. (D.A.Lovett)

68. This was the S&DR goods shed also known as the Merchandising Station. It is now the entry point to Hopetown Darlington, and includes the Clocktower Café, a gift shop and a railway-themed digital exhibition. It has been used by the DRPS for displaying its collection of locomotives local to Darlington. Both this building and North Road station are Grade II listed and being restored as part of the current programme. In the yard are two yellow 1ft 8½in gauge Ruston Hornsby 4WDMs from the former Chemical and Insulating Works, Nickstream, Darlington.

The station site is currently divided into a single platform served by Northern Trains Tees Valley services between Bishop Auckland and Saltburn and vice-versa. This passes under the overall roof extending from the museum over the erstwhile carriage shed, but this section of the lengthy platform is now out of use, trains stopping at the eastern section, now accessed by a new entrance from North Road itself. The two former southern platforms are now part of the railway museum.

Darlington Hopetown goods depot closed on 3rd May 1965 whilst North Gate Coal Depot officially closed on 3rd April 1971 and became a private siding coal depot from 5th April 1971. (D.A.Lovett)

Skerne Bridge

69. Skerne Bridge is an original S&DR bridge and leads from North Road to Albert Hill, an industrial area where firms often had small shunters to work their sidings. On the left is the Albert Hill signal box which closed on 21st September 1969. This view is looking back on 7th May 1949. (J.W.Armstrong/ARPT)

4. North Road to Oak Tree Junction via Fighting Cocks

The line to Eaglescliffe originally ran across undeveloped land. Following the opening of the line between Darlington and Newcastle in 1844 by the Newcastle & Darlington Joint Railway, the line from North Road crossed it on the level at S&D Crossing.

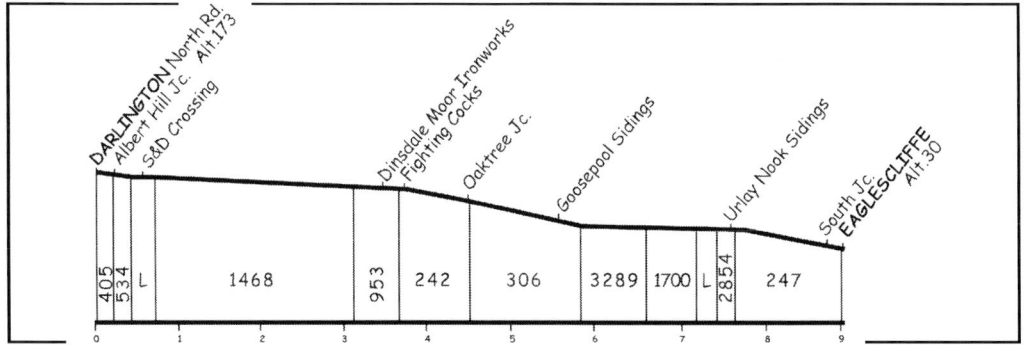

Gradient Profile of the original route from Darlington to Eaglescliffe via Fighting Cocks.

XXVI. The area east of North Road was dominated by various engineering companies when this 1896 map was published, all of which were rail served. The principal companies are detailed on the next page.

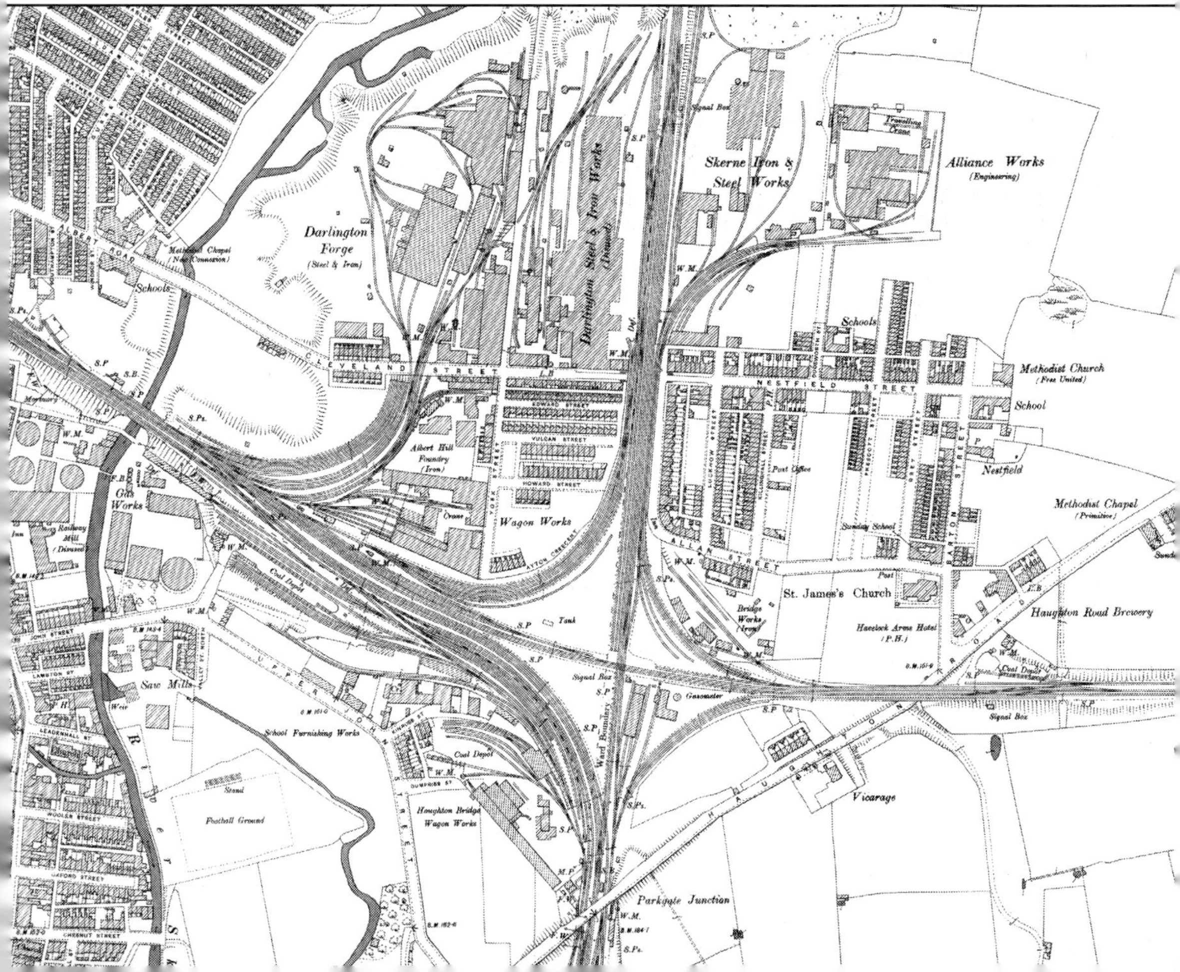

South Durham Iron Works

In 1854 work began on the construction of the South Durham Iron Works at Albert Hill which was becoming an industrial estate. Lines were also built into two adjoining businesses The Darlington Forge and John Harris's foundry. By 1859 three blast furnaces were at work. But by 1880 liquidators had been appointed to the ironworks and in 1886 the company was sold to the Darlington Forge Company.

The Darlington Forge Company

Opened in 1854, the company was originally owned by Cowans & Sheldon of Carlisle. In addition to railway work the company specialised in marine engineering. In 1875 it was described as the largest facility of its type in the UK. It was the second largest employer in Darlington after the NER.

It produced many of the parts for the great ocean liners including RMS *Titanic* and during WWI carried out work for the Admiralty as well as producing guns and tracks for tanks.

By the 1930s the decline in marine orders led to financial difficulties and temporary closure until the English Steel Corporation took a controlling interest. However, the outbreak of WWII saw a huge increase in workload and saw it employ some 2,000 people during the height of hostilities.

The company finally closed in 1967 resulting in the loss of some 650 jobs.

70. Darlington Forge had several tank engines including 0-4-0ST *Woodbank*, Black Hawthorn 387/1874 seen here in 1938. Other foundries and ironworks in this area had similar small shunters and for a short time John Harris built industrial engines in Hopetown. (J.W.Armstrong/ARPT)

John Harris's Foundry

John Harris was born in Cumberland in 1812. He became the permanent way engineer of the S&DR and for the construction of new lines in which the company was involved. He was one of the first PW engineers to use wooden sleepers in 1839, in place of the more commonly used stone blocks to which the rails were attached. By 1844 he was appointed a contractor to the S&DR with a 10 year contract to maintain and extend the company's permanent way. This allowed him to work for other railway companies and, in 1853, leased the Hopetown Foundry which specialised in producing cast rail chairs and wheels in conjunction with Thomas Summerson, with whom he patented improved railway wagon wheels in 1855.

John Harris died in 1871, Thomas Summerson had by then set up his own works at Abbey Hill Foundry to continue producing wheels and track components.

S&D Crossing

The opening of the Newcastle & Darlington Junction Railway north of Darlington in 1844 created the flat S&D Crossing with connecting lines being provided to allow access in four directions. The complex network around the S&D Crossing can be seen in map XXIV.

Regular passenger services on the original S&DR route between North Road (Albert Hill Junction) and Oak Tree Junction ceased on 1st July 1887, when trains were diverted through Darlington Bank Top station. However, the route remained available for freight traffic, diverted passenger trains and special workings.

Latterly known as the Fighting Cocks Branch, it was severed as a through route when Albert Hill Junction to Lingfield Lane closed on 21st May 1967, the short section over S&D Crossing having been singled in May 1956. Following the loss of the Paton's wool traffic, the line remained only at the eastern end served from Oak Tree Junction. The remaining line was lifted following the closure of the rail welding depot in 1988.

71. The S&DR made a famous crossing of the ECML on the level at Parkgate. In October 1964, BoBoDE class 24 no. D5170 was crossing, light engine, from west to east. (ARPT)

72. Class A8 4-6-2T no. 69891 brings a diverted passenger train from the Fighting Cocks line into Parkgate Junction. A8 locomotives were originally built as class H1 4-4-4T but were rebuilt in the 1930s, the extra driving wheels giving better adhesion. Behind the Parkgate signal box is the GNofER engine shed now preserved in a housing development. (J.Armstrong/ARPT)

The Croft Branch

The 3½ mile Croft Branch left the S&DR main line near Hill House, Albert Hill and travelled across Bank Top to the River Tees at Croft Bridge. The GNofER bought the branch from the S&DR for £20,000 but only used the Parkgate to Bank Top section, building their own station at Croft Spa where there was an alkaline spa with a bath house. The remaining line served what became known as Croft Goods. See Section 5 for information on this line.

Nestfield Industrial Area

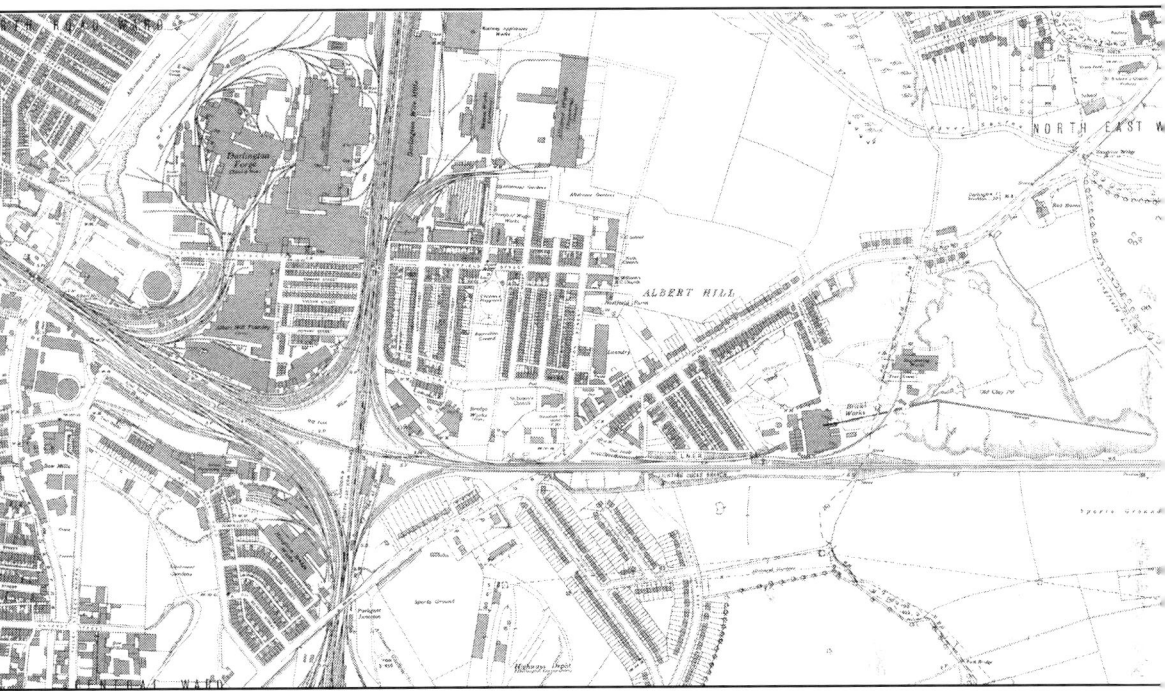

XXVII. The Nestfield Industrial Area is seen here in 1947, with its proliferation of engineering companies. After passing over the ECML at S&D Crossing, the line served several engineering and industrial concerns located in the Nestfield Industrial area between the ECML and S&DR lines to the north of the crossing all of which had rail connections.

The Skerne Iron Works plant on the Albert Hill side of the ECML was constructed in 1863. The company was already in existence and was known as Pease, Hutchinson & Ledward, Pease, moving to the new facility in 1864. Following the death of Walter Pease in 1872 the company was reorganised and became the Skerne Iron Works Company Ltd. It produced plates for the ship building industry, boilers and bridges. It produced a considerable number of wrought iron bridges for the NER. The company closed in 1882 and the site was later occupied by the Skerne Steel Wire Co.

Skerne Wire Works took over in 1893 the site of the former Skerne Iron Works. It was taken over by the Darlington Wire Mills in 1904. In 1964 the company was taken over by Sheffield based Aurora Gear and Engineering Co., before it disposed of the company in 1968.

The Railway Appliances Works was owned by Henry Williams Ltd. The company was formed in Glasgow in 1883, it established a base in Darlington in 1911. The company is a major supplier of signalling and other equipment to both the road, rail and energy industries and continues to operate from its base in Dodsworth Street, Darlington although it is no longer rail served.

In 1869 the Albert Hill Foundry was acquired by Thomas Summerson & Sons to produce points and switches for the railway industry. Summerson, born in 1810, became the Permanent Way Inspector of the S&DR in 1839. Specialising in points and crossings, by 1853 he was managing the Hopetown Foundry, which he subsequently purchased. In 1906 the company acquired the adjacent works of the Darlington Wagon & Engineering Company. Further expansion took place in 1909 with the acquisition of Barningham's Foundry, the home of the Darlington Iron Company.

In 1961 the company had 230 employees. The receivers were called in and although the foundry was saved by another company for a further nine years, the trackwork side of the business came to an end.

Alliance Works was opened in 1868 by brothers James and George Wilson, the company manufactured railway wheels. James was a partner in the Darlington Wagon Company whose works were nearby on York Street. The two companies amalgamated in 1884 and later took on bridge building work acquired following the closure of the Skerne Iron Company. After closure in 1905 the site was acquired by Blake Engineering and later by Metropolitan Carriage & Wagon Company until it closed the site around 1927.

Nestfield Engine Works and Nestfield Wagon Works were also rail served.

Haughton Road Industrial Area

The Haughton Road Industrial area can be seen on the previous map. The facilities included a tramway between the clay pit and brickworks with a siding into the engineering works. The Haughton Road area also contained several rail served works over the years. These included the NER (later LNER) Oil Gas Works and the Albert Hill Bridge Boiler Works.

Glico Petroleum Oil Depot was established in 1888 as the Gas Lighting Improvement Co. with its headquarters at London Wall and was well established by WWI when it was a major distributor of Carburine Motor Spirit. By the 1920s it was known as G.L.I.Co and became Glico Petroleum in 1926. In 1931 Glico merged with the Redline Motor Spirit Company, which was part of the Anglo-American Oil Company. In 1951 the company changed its name to Esso Petroleum Ltd. The facility at Darlington opened in 1927 stored fuel for onward distribution.

A coal depot known as Haughton Road was in use by 1839 until the end of the 19th century whilst Haughton Road brick works dated from around 1877, but, by 1914, was operating under the name of Blackett & Sons.

Paton & Baldwins is a company synonymous with knitting wools. Construction started on a new complex at Lingfield Point, two miles east of the town centre in August 1945. The site covered 107 acres, production starting in 1947 with the complex completed in 1951 at a cost of £7.5m. It became the largest wool factory in the world. Australian wool arrived by rail and was processed and made into balls for home knitting which also left the site by rail. Their shunter was a fireless locomotive 0-4-0F by W.Bagnall (2898/1948) now with the DRPS.

The factory remains open and is now owned by Coats, the company it merged with in 1961. It is no longer rail served; the siding agreement being terminated on 5th May 1972.

The Rural Council had loading docks served by the old line whilst the Dinsdale Wire & Steel Works opened in 1882. In 1931 W.H. Arnott, Young & Company took over the Dinsdale Wire & Steel works site as a scrapyard with new sidings provided. During the 1960s, many ex-BR steam engines were scrapped here. Arnott, Young was taken over by T.J. Thompson & Son in 1980 and the sidings at Fighting Cocks were operated by Dinsdale Metal Processors Limited until abolished in February 1983.

To the north of Fighting Cocks, the Dinsdale Moor Iron Works opened in 1860. It closed in 1954 resulting in further loss of traffic.

FIGHTING COCKS

↗ XXVIII. The station and goods yard are seen here during its goods only days in 1897. Although known as Fighting Cocks after the nearby public house of that name, which opened three years after the railway, it became a stopping place for early trains although there were no platforms nor passenger facilities. In November 1846, Bradshaw recorded the station here as Middleton & Dinsdale after the two nearest villages. The station had been rebuilt around 1860 and was renamed Fighting Cocks on 1st September 1866. The station lost its passenger services on 1st July 1887 when services were diverted via Darlington Bank Top and the new line via Dinsdale. Goods facilities survived until 9th March 1964. A lime and a coal depot were in use here by April 1830.

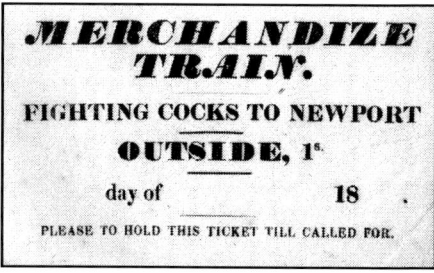

73. The original S&DR line went east to the north of the centre of Darlington to Middleton, Keso and Dinsdale. In this area was the public house, 'The Fighting Cocks' which served the S&DR as a station. (K.Taylor coll./ A.E.Young coll.)

74. Fighting Cocks station closed in 1887 and passenger services came from the south end of Bank Top station through to Dinsdale. This is the station on 10th May 1949. The stone construction on the up platform framed a passenger shelter. (LGRP/R. Humm coll.)

75. The goods yard became a scrapyard run by Arnott, Young Ltd. The line was severed at the western end leaving a short line from Oak Tree Junction. until the 1980s. On 27th August 1967, the wreckers were at work with two Ivatt 2-6-0 locomotives awaiting their attention.

Just south of Fighting Cocks was the Middleton & Dinsdale Gas Works which opened in 1871 and was served by a single siding. The siding arrangement dated from April 1892.

Charles Frederick Ingram, described as a 'railway wagon builder and repairer', took over the sidings for Ingrams Wagon Works by an agreement signed on 9th May 1921. This agreement ran until 5th April 1945.

Middleton Iron Works operated four blast furnaces on its site powered by a stationary steam engine and had an internal narrow gauge railway system for moving slag. Opened in 1864 it closed in 1931 with the works finally being demolished in 1947. The site was later used by BR as a Rail Welding Depot where rails were welded into 600ft lengths. It opened in 1958 it closed in 1988. (ARPT)

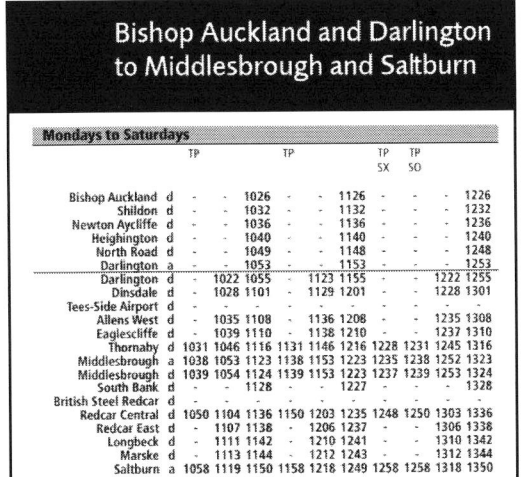

2023 Timetable extracts for the Bishop Line.

XXIX. This 1947 map shows the former Middleton Iron Works site just before it was demolished. The line to the southwest is the 1887 'new' line from Darlington South Junction, which joins the original line at Oak Tree Junction on the right. The old line was lifted in 1988.

Oak Tree Junction

The old and new lines joined here opening on 1st July 1887. The junction took its name from a nearby public house. From here the line continues to Eaglescliffe, Yarm, Stockton and Middlesbrough.

5. North Road to Croft via Darlington Bank Top

Today the line from Bishop Auckland and Shildon joins the East Coast Main Line at Parkgate Junction. All trains serve Darlington Bank Top where passengers to and from the main line services can change to join services to Bishop Auckland or Saltburn via Middlesbrough.

The S&DR opened a branch line to Croft from North Road on 27th October 1829, which ran through the future site of Bank Top station.

XXX. Darlington engine shed, seen in 1947, showing both the roundhouse and the added 1939 straight shed. Located north of Bank Top station, the shed was on the east side of the main line. It supplemented an earlier GNofER shed, opened in 1841, near the flat crossing. A new roundhouse was authorised in 1864 capable of holding 18 locomotives access being via a 42ft 3ins turntable. This sufficed until 1939 when a new seven road through shed, which could be accessed from the north or south, was built. A 70ft turntable was erected in the shed yard. It operated under BR's North Eastern Region using the shed code 51A (1948-1966). It usually had around 100 locomotives allocated to it.

A diesel depot opened on the opposite side of the main line in 1957. The steam sheds were demolished following the end of steam operation in the area in 1966.

➔ 76. There was another railway works at Darlington. This was at Springfield a few miles north on the ECML and out of the scope of this book (see *Darlington to Newcastle* and *Darlington - Leamside - Newcastle*). To represent this works, here is a new metre gauge 2-6-4T locomotive from there on its way to Burma (Myanmar) and passing the Bank Top power station on 3rd October 1948. It is ST 768 (RSH 7347) last reported to be out of use at Makpalin on 23rd February 1999. ST 759 of this class (RSH 7320) was presented by the Myanmar authorities to the Beijing Railway Museum, China.
(J.W. Armstrong/ARPT)

Darlington TMD (Diesel Depot)

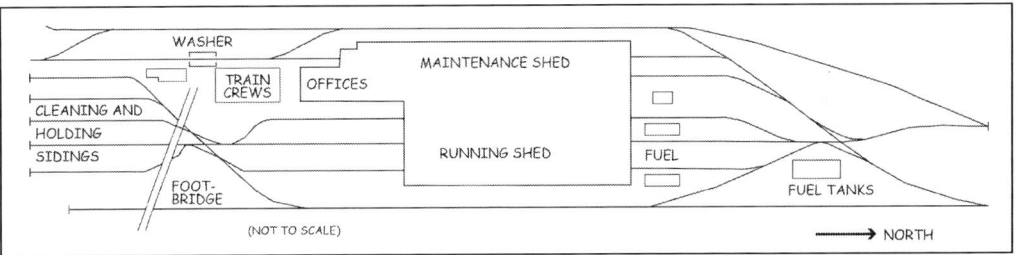

XXXI. Track plan of the Diesel Depot. This stood to the north of the station, which was to the left of the diagram. (Middleton Press)

77. With the arrival of diesel multiple units, a new depot was built on the western side of the approach to Darlington Bank Top station, north of the power station whose cooling towers are just visible in the right background. This view of the north end of the depot is looking south. It had opened on 17th September 1957 and the steam and diesel facilities worked in tandem for the next nine years, the two being linked by a footbridge for staff use. The depot retained the 51A shed code after the steam shed closed until 1973 when it became DN.

There was a three-road running shed and a two-road repair shed each capable of holding four-car diesel multiple units under cover. Four fuelling points were provided along with a washing plant. Staff accommodation was provided by a two-storey building to accommodate some 130 staff.

The diesel depot closed on 14th May 1984, supplanted by the existing Heaton DMU depot, Newcastle and was demolished in about 1990. Local DMU services operated by Northern are provided by Darlington based train crews with some units being serviced overnight in the bay platforms at the south end of the station. (ARPT)

Darlington MPD

78. Darlington steam shed was situated just to the northeast of Bank Top station. This is a view of the turntable and shed looking north in 1960. The locomotive line-up includes classes J27 0-6-0, B1 4-6-0 and L1 2-6-4T. The Shed Master's office was on the first floor of the office block, with the Running Foreman's office below him. (R.R.Darsley)

79. Even in the last week of steam, the shed always had a main line locomotive on standby in case of failure. Usually, a 4-6-2 was sitting on the turntable so that it could leave for the north or the south with a push of the turntable. Two of Darlington's Pacifics here were A1 4-6-2 no. 60124 *Kenilworth* and 60145 *St. Mungo*. (R.Humm coll.)

DARLINGTON BANK TOP

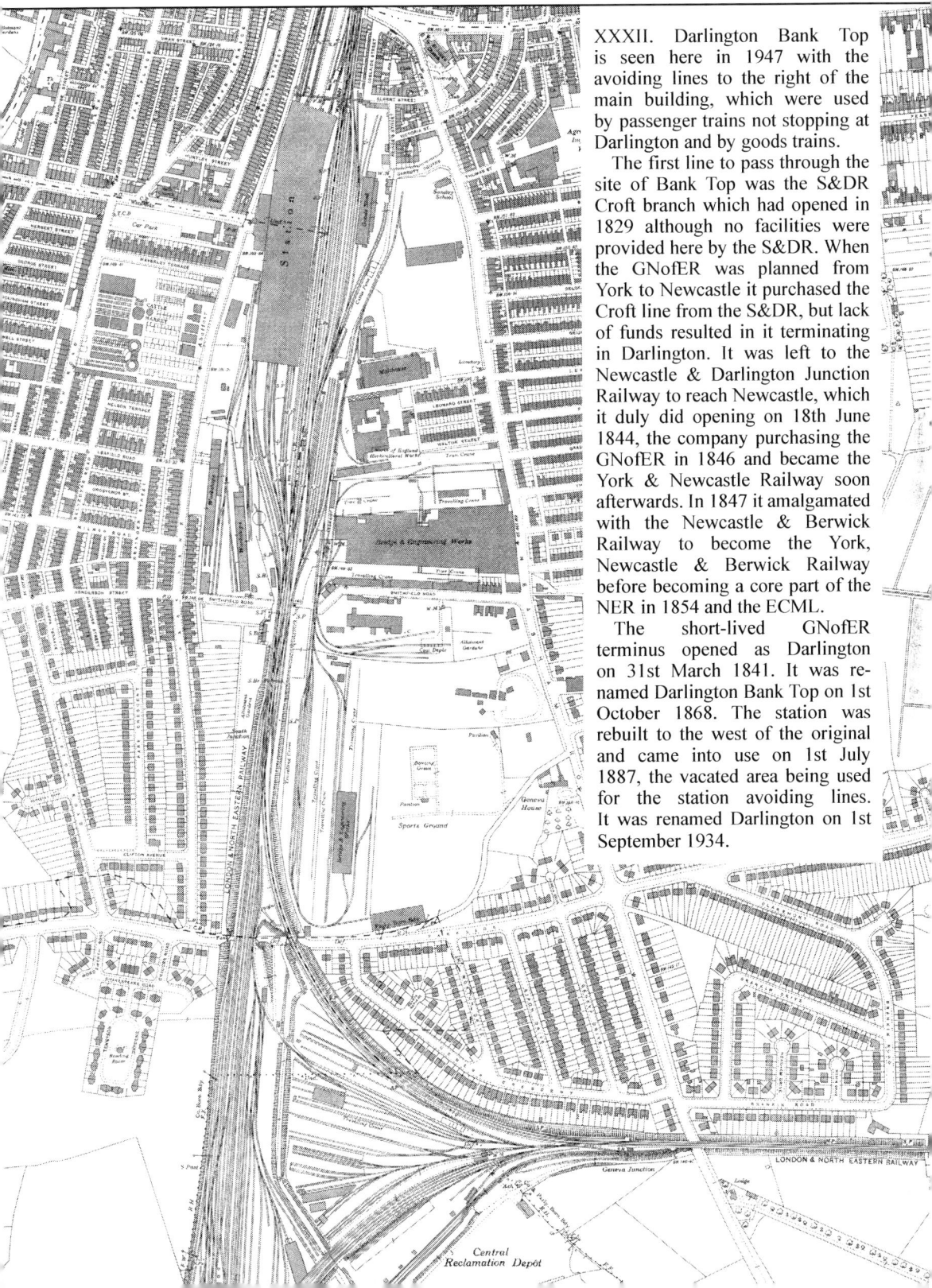

XXXII. Darlington Bank Top is seen here in 1947 with the avoiding lines to the right of the main building, which were used by passenger trains not stopping at Darlington and by goods trains.

The first line to pass through the site of Bank Top was the S&DR Croft branch which had opened in 1829 although no facilities were provided here by the S&DR. When the GNofER was planned from York to Newcastle it purchased the Croft line from the S&DR, but lack of funds resulted in it terminating in Darlington. It was left to the Newcastle & Darlington Junction Railway to reach Newcastle, which it duly did opening on 18th June 1844, the company purchasing the GNofER in 1846 and became the York & Newcastle Railway soon afterwards. In 1847 it amalgamated with the Newcastle & Berwick Railway to become the York, Newcastle & Berwick Railway before becoming a core part of the NER in 1854 and the ECML.

The short-lived GNofER terminus opened as Darlington on 31st March 1841. It was renamed Darlington Bank Top on 1st October 1868. The station was rebuilt to the west of the original and came into use on 1st July 1887, the vacated area being used for the station avoiding lines. It was renamed Darlington on 1st September 1934.

DARLINGTON.

A telegraph station.

HOTELS.—King's Head, family and commercial; Omnibuses to and from every train.

DARLINGTON, a market town in Durham, situated at the foot and side of a hill on the banks of the river Skern, over which there is a handsome bridge, has a population of 15,781 engaged in the cotton, flax, and worsted mills, foundries, and glass works. The principal ornament of this town is its church, which is built in the form of a cross, with a tower and spire rising from the centre to the height of nearly 200 feet and was founded in 1160 by Bishop Pudsey, in whose palace Princess Margaret stopped in 1504 on her way to Scotland. Many improvements have been made in this town, and considerable manufactures are carried on in linen, wool, and cotton. There are also several mills in its immediate neighbourhood. In 1805 a mineral spring was discovered near Darlington, which has gained much celebrity for its efficacy in scorbutic complaints. The celebrated bull "Comus" was sold here for £1,050. In the vicinity are Oxen Hall with the High Kettle salt springs. Bushell Hill, from whence York cathedral can be seen, *Blackwell*, the seat of R. H. Allan, Esq., and of his late brother the antiquarian, and *Southend*, J. Pease, Esq.

80. Grade II* listed Bank Top station was opened on 1st July 1887 (note: a small percentage of Grade II buildings are labelled as Grade II*, as they are judged to be of particular importance or special interest). It was designed and built by NER staff T.E.Harrison and William Bell, and cost £81,000. The Italianate tower is on the Victoria Road entrance on the west side of the station. Besides the clock it had a station bell cast in 1886 and preserved from September 1983 on the station concourse. The photograph, taken on 30th July 1952, shows the trolley bus wires in Park Lane. From horse trams in 1880, the Corporation moved to electric trams in 1904 and trolleybuses in 1926. The five-route system closed on 31st July 1957. Further details can be found in our album *Darlington Trolleybuses - including the Tramways*. (LGRP/R.Humm coll.)

81. There are currently four platforms at the station with platform 1 being the main platform for southbound departures and platform 4 for northbound services, but both platforms are signalled for bi-directional working. Platforms 2 & 3 are the bay platforms at the south end used mainly by terminating services from Saltburn. The Grade II listed station is due to undergo renovation in the lead up to the 2025 Anniversary, with the construction of two new platforms proposed to serve the avoiding lines.

Darlington Bank Top station was, under its huge roof, basically an island platform. It also had avoiding lines that ran outside the station walls. Here Gresley's experimental water tube boiler locomotive class W1 no. 10000 heads south with a train signalled for no. 1 platform in 1929. Strictly speaking the locomotive was a 4-6-2-2. It was rebuilt with a conventional boiler in October 1937 and became no. 60700. (J.W.Armstrong/ARPT)

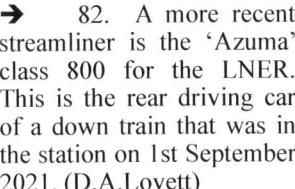
← Extract from *Bradshaws Guide*, 1866.

→ 82. A more recent streamliner is the 'Azuma' class 800 for the LNER. This is the rear driving car of a down train that was in the station on 1st September 2021. (D.A.Lovett)

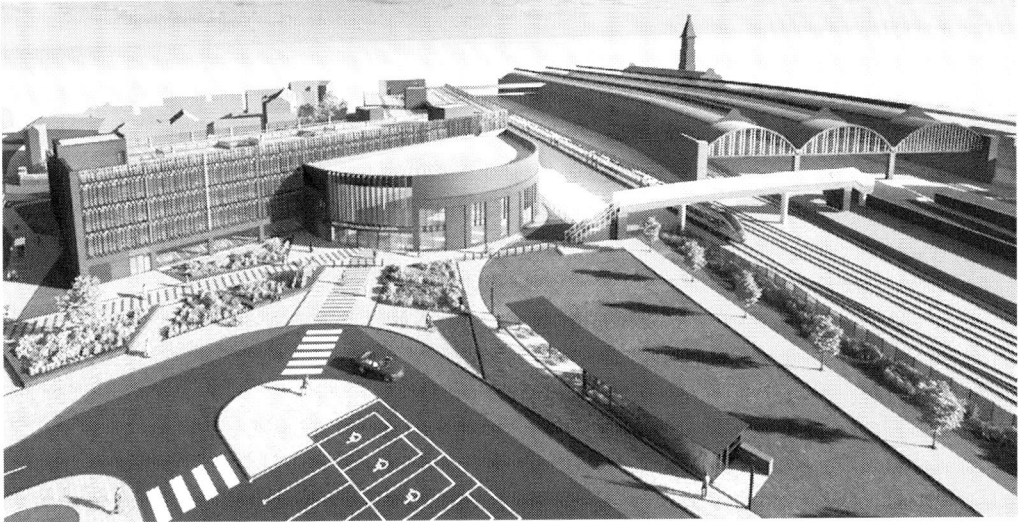
83. Work started on 1st August 2022 to provide a new transport hub at Bank Top station with more platforms, better interchange and a multi-storey car park. Delays in raising the money and getting planning permission means it will not be completed until 2026, after the S&DR celebrations. (Napper Architects Co.)

84. The south side of the station had bays for local trains. 2-6-2T no. 82028 stands in platform 2 on a Saltburn train. No. 82028 had a short life of 12 years (December 1954 to September 1966) compared with the 60 years of class G5 0-4-4T no. 67284 present off a Middleton-in-Teesdale push/pull train. (Initial Photographics)

85. LNER class B13 4-6-0 no. 761 (NER class S) was alongside Darlington South Box on 4th June 1933. Built in June 1906, it was withdrawn to service stock in September 1934. It survived as a counter pressure test locomotive at Darlington North Road Works paint shop until May 1951. Renumbered no. 1699 in October 1946, it was moved to Rugby Testing Station after nationalisation and was scrapped at Crewe Works. The 140-lever mechanical signal box was opened in 1905 and replaced by a 155-lever power box on 6th May 1939. (W.Rogerson/R.Humm coll.)

Cleveland Bridge UK Ltd

The factory and sidings of the Cleveland Bridge company can be seen in map XXXII, opposite picture 78. Opened in 1877 the company specialised in large steel structures and became a world-famous bridge building company. Their work included the bridge crossing Victoria Falls in Zimbabwe, the Sydney Harbour Bridge, the Bosporus Europe – Asia road bridge, the Tyne Bridge and the Tees Transporter Bridge amongst many others. Its Smithfield Road works were served by sidings on the east side of the ECML just south of Darlington Bank Top station. Cleveland Bridge notably had the last working steam engine in the Darlington area, Peckett 0-4-0 Saddle Tank *Adam*, which was withdrawn from regular use by the early-1970s and thereafter kept 'in reserve' until disposed of in 1977 to the Cambrian Railways Society at Oswestry for preservation (now the Cambrian Heritage Railway). Smithfield Road works closed in December 1981 and was replaced the following month by a new factory in Yarm Road, Darlington, served by a new siding on the north side of the line at Maidendale, near milepost 2 towards Dinsdale. Rail traffic ceased about 1993 and Maidendale siding was removed in September 2021. Coincidentally, the company closed during the same month after it had gone into administration in July 2021.

Darlington South Junction

The former triangular junction was removed in 1969 and today only the curve to the Tees Valley line remains. The junction to the Croft Depot branch is shown at the bottom of map XXXII.

Using the northernmost junction of the triangle it was originally known as Polam Junction. The line opened from here to Oak Tree Junction on 1st July 1887 resulting in all passenger trains being diverted away from the old line to serve Darlington Bank Top station.

Triangular junction access from the south was gained from Snipe House Junction on the ECML to Geneva Junction on the S&DR where it was joined by the line from Darlington South Junction. The south side of the triangle, which lays beyond the reclamation yard, opened in 1931 and closed on 6th October 1969.

A Central Reclamation Depot stood in the triangle and had large overhead cranes for dealing with track recovery. It opened in 1931 and closed in 1966. The site was used for sorting out reclaimed track materials such as sleepers, chairs, fishplates and rails and on receipt would be graded for further use, reworking or scrapping. The facility was equipped with workshops including blacksmiths forges and a foundry. A large overhead gantry crane was provided some 560ft in length and its 59ft span served two tracks with a central storage area. The magnetic crane was used for lifting lengths of rail. The reclaimed material was sent out by rail for further use within the North Eastern Region Engineers area.

CROFT

XXXIII. The ECML runs through the centre of the map and shows Croft Spa station to the north of the road running east to west. On the map the Croft Depot branch is to the left of the main line. The Coal depot branch is also to the left of the main line and shows the link to the gas works as well as the coal facilities. The gradient profile for the short Croft branch is shown alongside. (Middleton Press)

Access to the Croft Depot branch was via Croft Yard, which initially served a coal depot in the village of Croft-on-Tees. Coal from the pits around Shildon was transported to the depot that opened in October 1829. Coal Docks were provided at Croft which gave the collieries access to the markets of Yorkshire (which was at that time on the opposite bank of the River Tees).

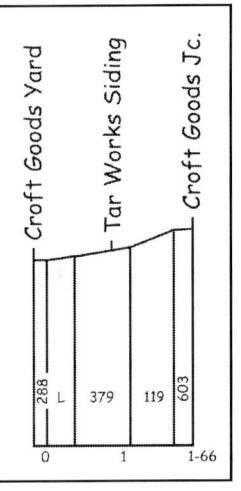

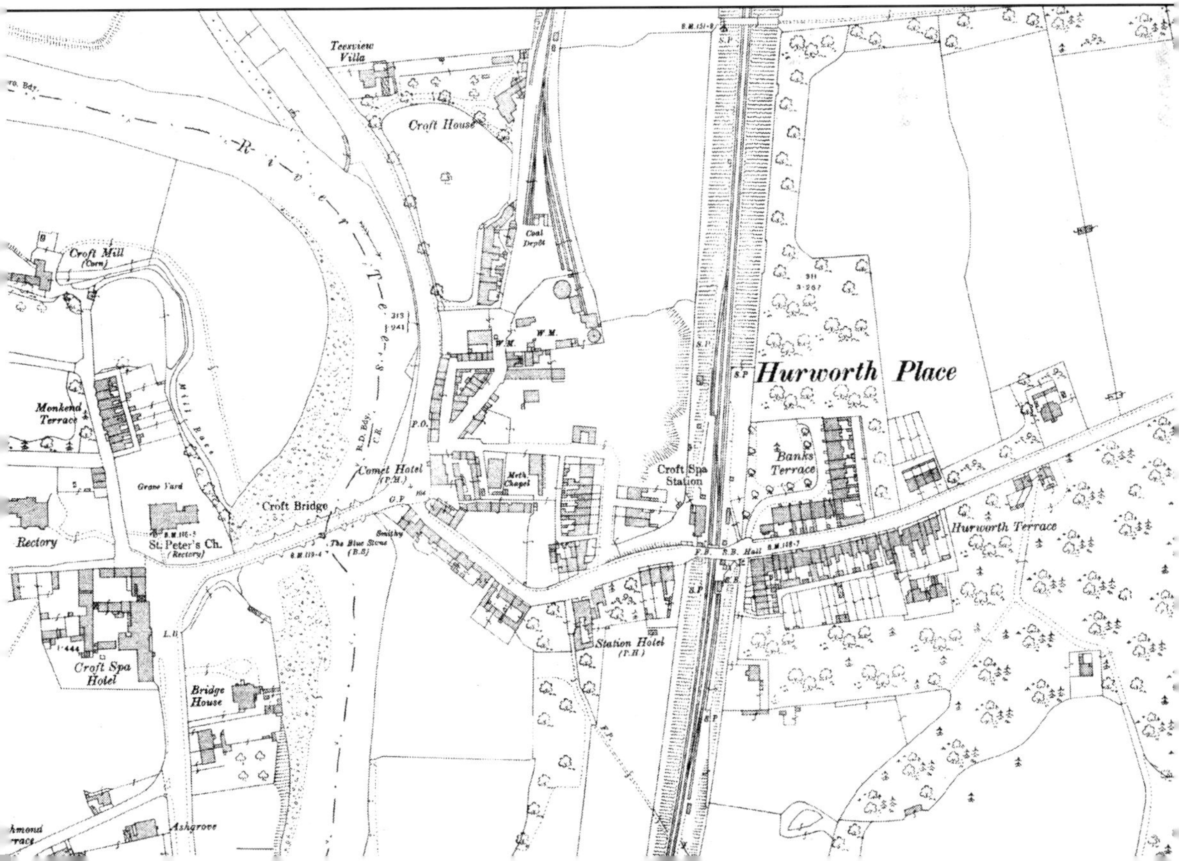

86. A photograph, taken in 1960, shows class J27 0-6-0 no. 65860 shunting the Croft Depot sidings with the line looking out to the north. The line closed in 1964. In their time the coal drops dealt with 10,000 tons of coal a year. (R.Coulthard/ARPT)

87. At Croft, coal was transferred to boats on the River Tees or pack horses for onward transit over Croft Bridge until the opening of the line between York and Darlington in 1841 resulted in this being no longer necessary. Class J94 0-6-0ST no. 68043 was at the terminus and gas holder in April 1964. Thomas Ness had a gas works at Black Banks.

For a short period, September-December 1833, a passenger service was also operated, and again from 1st February 1837, when William Walton was given a year's contract to run the service.

The GNofER purchased the branch from the S&DR and utilised it as part of its main line then being built between York and Darlington which opened on 31st March 1841.

The southern section of the old line was retained as a separate branch from a new junction at Croft Junction just south of Darlington South Junction. It closed to goods traffic on 27th April 1964 following closure of the tar distillery linked to the gas works which it also served.

A new Croft station was opened on the GNofER main line on 31st March 1841. Renamed Croft Spa on 1st October 1896, after 15th September 1958 it was served only by Richmond branch trains to and from Darlington Bank Top and finally closed to passengers on 3rd March 1969 when services to Richmond ceased. (D. Tyreman)

6. Darlington South Junction to Oak Tree Junction via Dinsdale

This line was opened by the NER on 1st July 1887 allowing closure to passenger traffic of the original S&DR line from North Road to Oak Tree Junction via Fighting Cocks.

DINSDALE

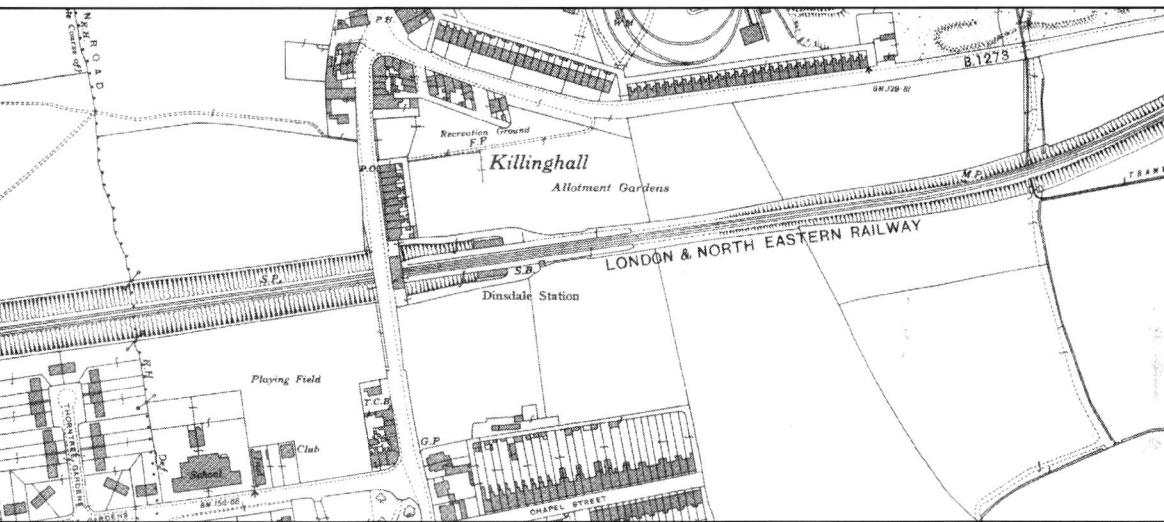

XXXIV. Dinsdale station in 1947 with the line entering the station in a cutting. The booking office was located adjacent to the road bridge.

Opened on 1st July 1887 this was a replacement for Fighting Cocks station, which was closed on the same date and located some ½ mile to the north on the original S&DR route. It served Dinsdale Spa that had been established in 1797 but which was sold in 1914 for residential use.

88. John Lambton, the 1st Earl of Durham, was drilling for coal and found a sulphur spring worth developing by building the Dinsdale Spa Hotel in 1829. Dinsdale station was convenient but the hotel had a varied career and is now residential apartments. The station buildings alongside the bridge over the railway were photographed on 11th April 1967 with the up platform for west-bound trains. (R.Goad/ARPT)

89. This is the Dinsdale down station platform for Stockton and Middlesbrough. The station remains open and is served by a Northern service to and from Middlesbrough and Saltburn plus Darlington and Bishop Auckland. The decoration in the brickwork was a pleasant style. The station buildings were demolished around 1973, being replaced by basic 'bus stop' style shelters.
(Photomatic/
A.E.Young coll.)

90. Dinsdale station with class A8 4-6-2T no. 69856 passing on an eastbound Stockton train going on to Saltburn. The station buildings on the bridge can be seen behind the train. (J.W.Armstrong/ARPT)

91. DMU no. 142021 is in the former yellow livery of the Tyne & Wear PTE on a train to Whitby via Middlesbrough in 1998. This class of 'Pacer' DMU was made with Leyland bus parts and a Leyland 4-wheel frame.
(J.Spencer Gilkes/
Colour-Rail.com)

7. Oak Tree Junction to Yarm and Stockton

XXXV. A map showing the original S&DR lines to both Yarm and Stockton via Eaglescliffe. The Stockton and Yarm branches split near the current Allens West station. Yarm business owners contributed significantly to the funding of the S&DR and, like the Darlington business, ensured that the S&DR served them both rather than avoiding them with a more direct route between Shildon and Stockton. Both Stockton and Yarm S&DR stations were relegated to goods station status and replaced by new stations. (Middleton Press)

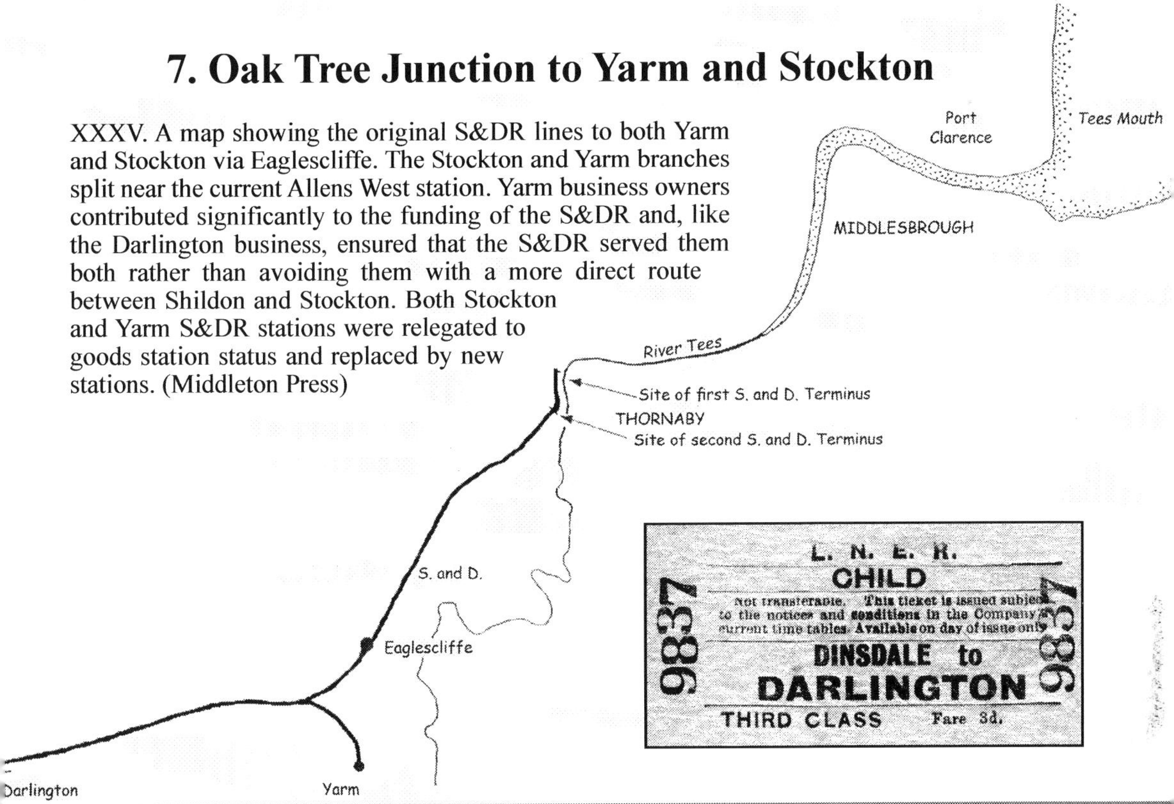

TEESSIDE AIRPORT

XXXVI. Teesside Airport station was situated alongside the A67 on the northern edge of the airport. Construction of an RAF airfield began here in 1938 and became operational from 15th January 1941. Officially known as RAF Middleton St. George, it was known locally as Goosepool

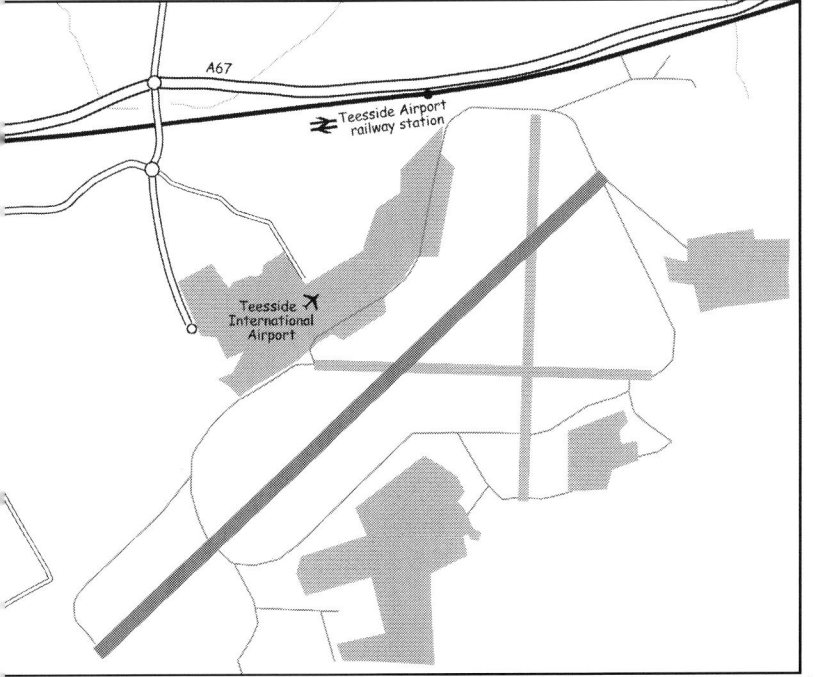

and was used by bomber squadrons. It passed to the Royal Canadian Air Force in October 1942 until the end of the war. In 1945 it became an RAF training station. The RAF departed in 1964 and work began on converting the airfield to civilian use as Teesside Airport, which opened that April. It was renamed Teesside International Airport in 1987. Between 2004 and 2019 it was known as Durham Tees Valley Airport before reverting to its former name. This station opened on 3rd October 1971 to serve the developing Teesside Airport. (Middleton Press)

92. Teesside Airport was Middleton St. George airfield in Military days. This was the Control Tower in 1964 shortly after it became commercial airport. Since then, it has had a chequered career though currently there is a plan to develop a business park alongside. (Northern Echo archives/coll. R.R.Darsley)

93. The station was owned by the airport but was not very convenient for the terminal and this was reflected in the very low passenger numbers. It was handed over to BR on 3rd October 1971. Due to the condition of the footbridge, it was decided in December 2017 that trains would stop only on the Darlington (up) bound platform, the one nearest the airport terminal building. In May 2021, the service was reduced to one train a week. The only west-bound train to stop was the 14.25 Hartlepool to Darlington on Sundays. This provided the parliamentary service needed to avoid having to go through the legal closure process. However, concern for the state of the platform and footbridge led to the total closure of the station with the last trains calling on 24th May 2022. (J.W.Armstrong/ARPT)

94 On 26th September 1972 two trains in the station was the maximum 'busyness' and may be then only one would ever stop! (A.E.Young)

Goosepool (1925 Centenary Celebrations)

Located at Goosepool, ½ mile east of the present day Teesside Airport station, a large covered grandstand was built on the north side of the line for the 1925 celebrations marking the S&DR 100th Anniversary. The Duke and Duchess of York (later King George VI and Queen Elizabeth) were in attendance to view a major procession of locomotives and rolling stock on 2nd July 1925. The participating trains were assembled at Stockton and represented both historical and the latest developments from the four Grouping companies, which had been formed only two years previously at the Grouping in 1923. Travelling past the grandstand the participants made for Fighting Cocks where dispersal was arranged, many going forward to Faverdale wagon works, Darlington, where the celebratory exhibition was held (see photo 52).

URLAY NOOK

XXXVII. Urlay Nook gave access to a chemical factory, chromium works and the Royal Naval stores. The public goods sidings on the Down side were closed on 2nd November 1964. A 1954 map shows the rail connections into the Royal Navy Depot. The short-lived Allen's Curve to the Leeds Northern line is marked as Old Railway.

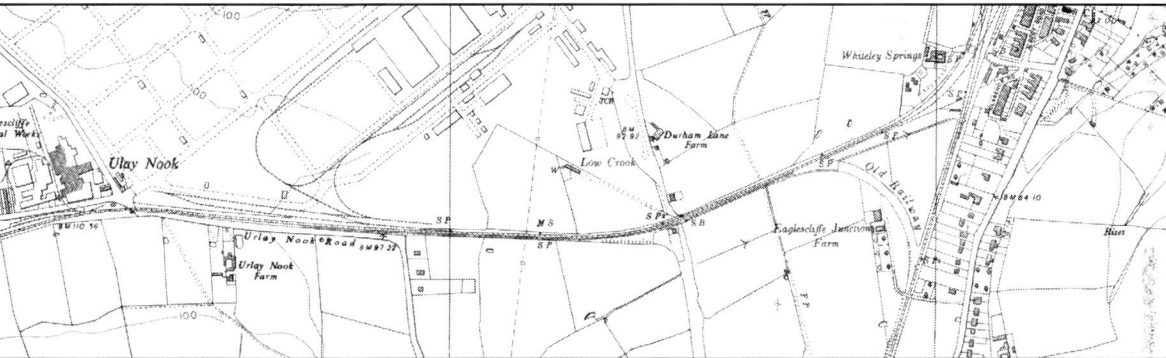

ALLENS WEST

XXXVIII. Located near the site of the original S&DR Yarm station, it opened during WWII as an unadvertised staff halt to serve the nearby Royal Navy stores depot. The depot opened in 1930 and once employed some 2,000 people. The halt first appeared in the Working Timetable for 4th October 1943. The site was used as a back-up airfield in WWII and was used to dismantle aircraft for a period. At one time there were extensive internal sidings connected to the S&DR line, which were worked by two industrial locomotives. In August 1975, they were used to stable locomotives for the S&DR 150 Celebrations. The site closed in 1997 and the buildings were subsequently demolished becoming a housing estate.

Allens West became a public station to serve new housing developments nearby on 4th October 1971. This 2023 map shows the position of Allens West.
(Middleton Press)

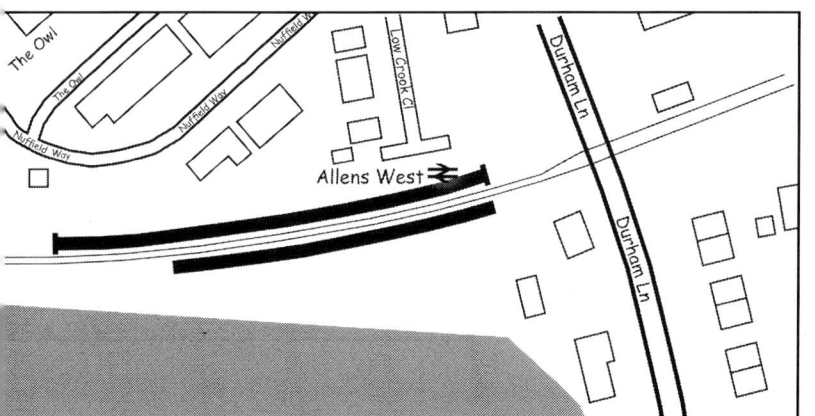

95. Allens West was built as an unadvertised station to serve the military 1940s estate of the same name. After the war, the site was Metal Reclamation Unit no. 2, recovering aluminium from scrap planes. From 1990 it was a Royal Navy Spare Parts store. The depot closed in 1997 to be replaced by an industrial park and housing. The station was handed over to BR in 1948. (R.Humm coll.)

96. Class L1 2-6-4T no. 67762 is heading for Saltburn via Stockton in March 1958. It is a very clean locomotive and this could be a running-in duty after a Darlington works visit. (J.W.Armstrong/ARPT)

97. Allens West station and crossing were refurbished in April 2013. In 2019 there was a proposal for another major housing scheme in the area. (D.A.Lovett)

Yarm Branch
YARM (S&DR)
Yarm Branch End

➔ XXXIX. The S&DR Yarm station and branch opened on 10th October 1825. The 1855 map refers to the station on the S&DR main line as Yarm, but it was also known as Yarm Branch End. The branch conveyed coal to depots established on privately owned land. The branch was closed on 16th June 1862 and abandoned in 1870 following the transfer of coal traffic to the nearby Yarm station on the Leeds Northern Railway (LNR), which had opened on 25th May 1852. Below is a simplified diagram showing the lines that have served Yarm over the years.

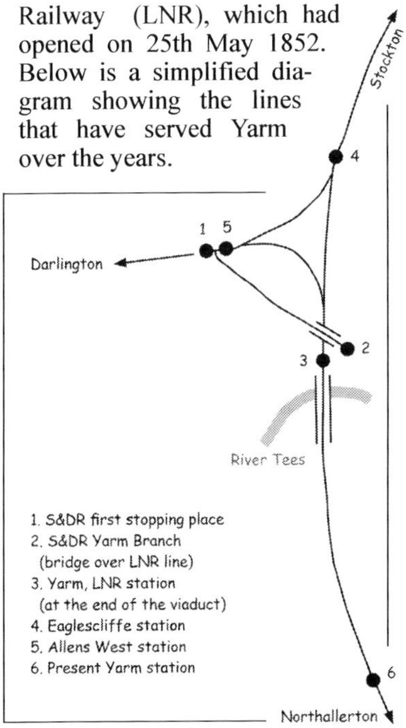

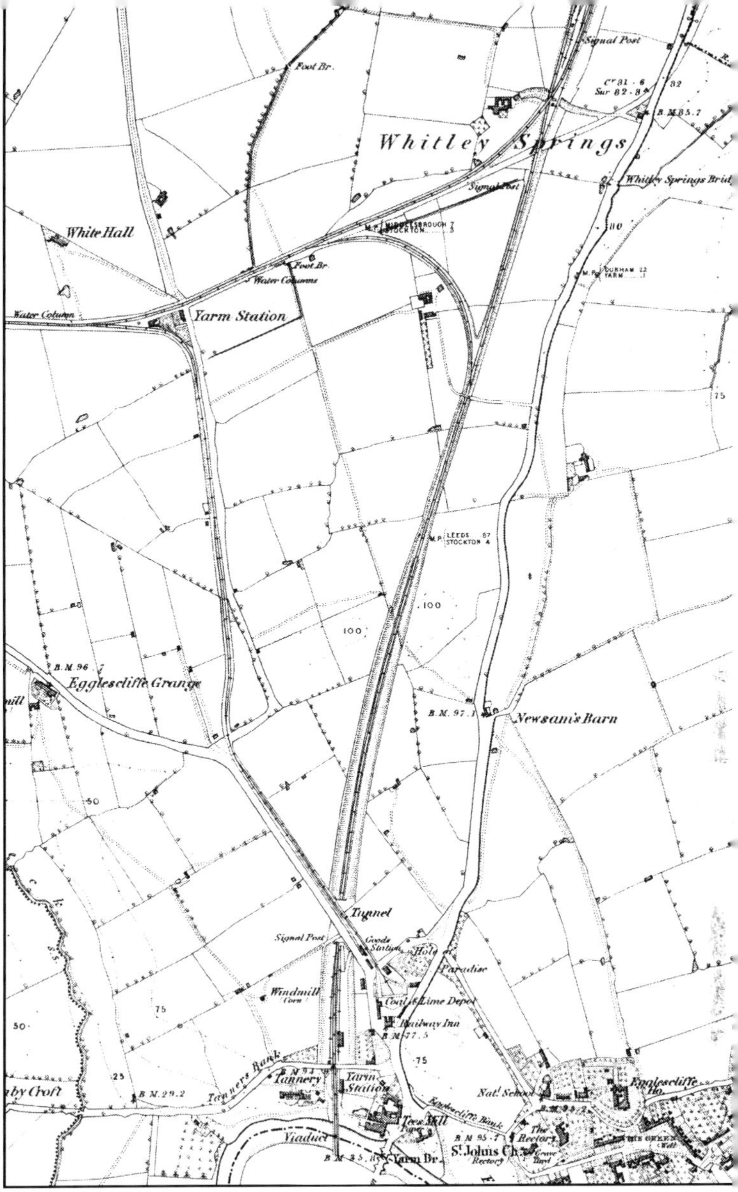

1. S&DR first stopping place
2. S&DR Yarm Branch (bridge over LNR line)
3. Yarm, LNR station (at the end of the viaduct)
4. Eaglescliffe station
5. Allens West station
6. Present Yarm station

Yarm Depots

98. A public house known as 'The New Inn' opened in October 1825 and served as the booking office for the horse-drawn passenger services, which commenced on 16th October 1826. The pub was the first ever railway pub and still exists as the 'Cleveland Bay'. The passenger coach *Union* worked on the branch. The passenger service officially ceased on 7th September 1833, but was occasionally run thereafter on specials and Sunday trains. The area of the coal and lime depots was known as the 'Hole of Paradise', and is now a block of residential apartments. The coal merchants house is now the only surviving reminder of the S&DR facilities at Yarm. The magnificent diorama is by Bill Ramage. (W.Ramage)

99. The 'George & Dragon' was another pub in Yarm of significance to the S&DR, for it was here on 12th February 1820 that the proposers first met to discuss the whole project of the S&DR. Thomas Meynell of Yarm presided over the meeting in the Commercial room, laid the first rail on 23rd May 1822 and went on to be Chairman of the S&DR. (R.Humm coll.)

Yarm (NER)

100. Immediately west of the Yarm branch divergence, a southbound curve to the Leeds Northern Railway opened with that line in 1852. Known as the Allens Curve, its use was short-lived, however, being used mainly for iron ore traffic from Rosedale to Ferryhill iron works before closure in about 1879.

The LNR became part of the North Eastern Railway before the S&DR. The NER station was just west of the Yarm Depots and immediately north of the dramatic Yarm viaduct, and here a NER 2-4-0 is on a down passenger train. The print has been touched up rather heavily but it appears to be a Tennant class (E5). These locomotives were designed by a committee who, for once produced a pedigree horse rather than a camel! This station was closed by BR on 4th January 1960 with housing now in the former goods yard. The present Yarm station, a platform and bus shelter affair, was opened on 19th February 1996, 1⅛ miles further south. (R.Humm coll.)

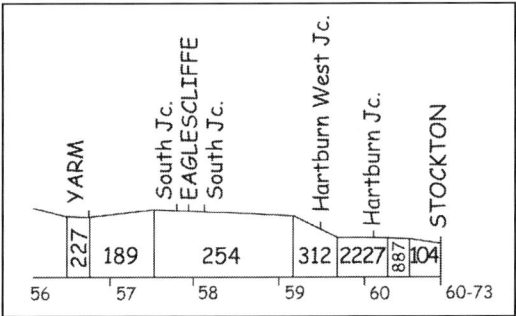

101. Yarm viaduct has a freight train hauled by an unidentified WD class 2-8-0 going north. The date is unknown but the two lorries, an AEC and possibly an Atkinson, put it in the mid- to late-1950s. The viaduct is 760 yards long with 43 arches. Built by Thomas Grainger and John Bourne of Edinburgh, it took three years to complete using 7.5 million bricks.
(R.Goad coll./ARPT)

The gradient profile of the Leeds Northern line from the former Yarm station to Stockton.

Timetable extract for services between Darlington and Saltburn 1961.

EAGLESCLIFFE

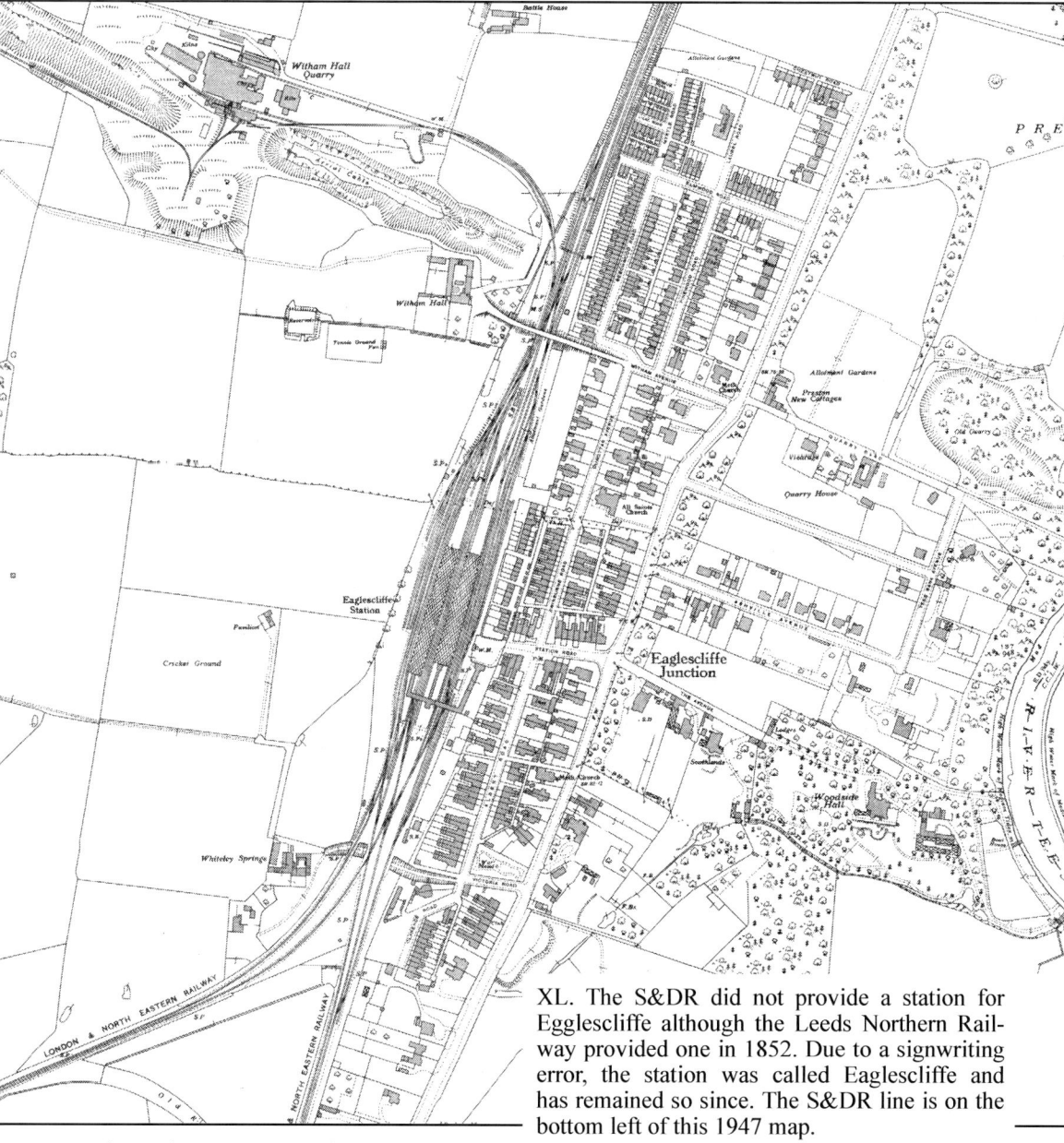

XL. The S&DR did not provide a station for Egglescliffe although the Leeds Northern Railway provided one in 1852. Due to a signwriting error, the station was called Eaglescliffe and has remained so since. The S&DR line is on the bottom left of this 1947 map.

The station was renamed Eaglescliffe Junction between 1852 and 1853, and Preston Junction from the following year. This name remained in place until 1st February 1878 when it became Eaglescliffe Junction again. In 1880 the junction part of the name was removed with the station becoming plain Eaglescliffe.

To cope with traffic, a new island platform (nos 3/4) opened at Eaglescliffe station, on the west side in 1894, but this was closed in 1969 when the Eaglescliffe layout was rationalised, all trains thereafter calling at the present east side island platform (nos 1/2).

102. NER class Q (D17/2) 4-4-0 no. 1930 leaves Eaglescliffe with a Down Express in May 1923. No. 1930 was the last of class built in 1897 and withdrawn in November 1933. Both north and south signal boxes closed in February and March 1969 respectively with control transferred to Bowesfield signal box. The down sidings served a Bass Beer distribution depot. (Photomatic/R.Humm coll.)

103. A view from the footplate of class A4 no. 60004 hauling an RCTS special on 19th September 1965. This locomotive was originally named *Great Snipe* in the series of fast flying birds but in 1941 it was renamed *William Whitelaw*. In 1965 the station was still a busy interchange. Visible across the station are a 'Peak' (Class 45) on express passenger, a class 101 DMU on a local, and Class 40 and class 24 on freight. (ARPT)

104. Class G5 0-4-4T no. 67343 is on the 3.30pm from West Hartlepool, all stations to Northallerton in 1956. All 110 of these sturdy locomotives saw more than 50 years of service over the whole of the North Eastern territories yet not one was preserved. The G5 Locomotive Co. Ltd. is building a replica at the Hackworth Industrial Park, Shildon, which is part of the old wagon works. Eaglescliffe lost its goods facilities on 6th July 1964. (J.W.Armstrong/ARPT)

105. DMU no. 143605 is the train to Bishop Auckland via Darlington on 29th June 1989. The SCG gearboxes on this class were unreliable and were replaced with Voith hydraulic transmissions from 1989. As they were changed their numbers had 600 added to them.

On 25th January 1853, the S&DR line was diverted from its original alignment adjacent to Preston Park and the grounds of Preston Hall (built in 1825, the same year the S&DR opened) to the west to lie alongside the recently-opened Leeds Northern line, forming a four-track section from the uniting of the two routes at Eaglescliffe South Junction for 1¾ miles before the lines diverged. The section was reduced to two tracks during the 1980s. The original S&DR route is now a footpath on the east side of the A135 (former A19) road in the grounds of Preston Hall which houses a museum including S&DR artefacts. The Teesside Small Gauge Railway (TSGR) has its miniature line in the north end of Preston Park.
(I.Worland/Colour-Rail.com)

106. Preston Park museum has several S&DR mementos. This photograph shows the style of the S&DR track with the rails fixed to stone blocks. It can be compared with more recent track with sleepers in the top right-hand corner. (coll. R.R.Darsley)

STOCKTON

Stockton saw the S&DR provide it with two early stations before the building of the current Stockton station, provided by the Leeds Northern Railway from 1852. However, the S&DR ceased to operate passenger trains into the town from 1848 when services were diverted to Middlesbrough.

Stockton S&DR

The S&DR's first station opened to goods traffic on 27th September 1825. It was used as the terminus of a horse drawn passenger service from 10th October 1825 and terminated adjacent to the Mariners Tavern on the quayside. Horse drawn services ceased on 7th September 1833 after which it was no longer used by passengers. The goods facilities closed here in 1967 although the line was not officially taken out of use until 9th October 1972. The original line terminated by the River Tees. It was here that coal was loaded onto barges for onward transit to where it was needed. This can be seen in map XXXV, opposite picture 89.

107. The old S&DR Stockton terminus is on the right with St John's level crossing signal box beyond. The building was converted into a weigh house for the S&DR in 1826. The Bridge Street building still exists and was used as a parcel department until the 1960s. It lost its rail use in 1970 and is currently a home for homeless men. (T.G.Hepburn/ R.Humm coll.)

108. Stockton S&DR terminus may have sold passenger tickets but it is more likely to have been the nearby pub known most commonly as 'The Teessider' now demolished. Passenger trains did run from here between 1833 and 1st July 1848. Here NER class J25 0-6-0 no.65689 is shunting the branch to the riverside. The loco was withdrawn from Stockton shed (51E) on 31st May 1954. (R.Humm coll.)

➜ XLI. A later map showing the fully developed rail network around Stockton and Middlesbrough. The second S&DR station in Bridge Road was located about ½ mile south of the original terminus, on the south side of St John's Crossing, where the S&DR first rail was ceremonially laid by Chairman Thomas Meynell on 23rd May 1822. The second station opened on 7th September 1833 when steam hauled services to Darlington commenced. Subsequently only wagons destined for the staithes crossed the road so that they could continue to be tipped into waiting ships at the original quayside terminus.

However, only primitive facilities existed until a proper station was provided in 1836. The second station closed to passengers in 1848, all services were thereafter diverted to Middlesbrough to which the S&DR had been extended from Bowesfield Junction on 27 December 1830 for horse-drawn trains, replaced by steam haulage in 1834. The main station in Stockton-on-Tees was opened in 1852 by the Leeds Northern Railway.

A weigh house and The Railway Tavern had opened in 1826, the latter serving as the booking office. Only the facility, The Cleveland Bay, at Yarm predated it (opened in October 1825). The Railway Tavern closed in 1869 and was later used as housing for railway employees; latterly it was celebrated as the 'First Railway Booking Office', which was not strictly true as it was preceded by other inns on the S&DR selling railway tickets. The building became a small museum during the S&DR 150 Anniversary in 1975 but is now used as a hostel and is Grade II listed.

South of St. John's crossing the goods shed, coal and lime depot were located along with the agent's house. Following cessation of passenger services, the site was developed by the NER into the town's major goods handling facility (later known as South Stockton) with a large building constructed in 1875. The site was further developed in the early 1960s becoming one of the seven North Eastern Region's goods concentration depots. It handled around 250 wagons per day. The site became home to National Carriers until the early 1980s. Much of the site was demolished in 1986. The line from Bowesfield Junction closed to all traffic on 28th September 1986. Much of the route was used for the A135 dual carriageway road known as 1825 Way which opened in 2003.

109. The Corporation Quay, Stockton, was the first loading point for the coal for London and abroad. Finished in 1825 it was not entirely satisfactory, as at low tide loaded ships would sometimes ground. In 1830 the S&DR constructed the Middlesbrough branch bypassing St. Johns Crossing and reaching the south side of the river, first with a suspension bridge and then in 1844 with an iron girder bridge. In its final year, on 13th August 1965, the Barclay 0-4-0ST *Kilmarnock* (814/1898) was shunting wagons of scrap. (J.Boyes/ARPT)

STOCKTON-ON-TEES.

A telegraph station.
HOTELS.—Black Lion; Vane Arms.
MARKET DAYS.—Wednesdays and Saturdays.
RACES in August.
FAIRS.—Wednesday before 13th March, 23rd November, last Wednesday in every month (for cattle).

A market town in the county of Durham, with a population of 13,357, employed in the coal and shipping trade. It is situated on the Tees, and celebrated for the manufacture of cloth and rope. The church of St. Thomas, Stone Bridge, and Town Hall are very fine buildings. Josiah Reed, Lord Mayor Crosby (whose obelisk is at Southwark), Ritson, and Alison were natives. The first bar of the line to Darlington was laid here in 1825, by F. Meynell, Esq.

Extract from *Bradshaws Guide*, 1866.

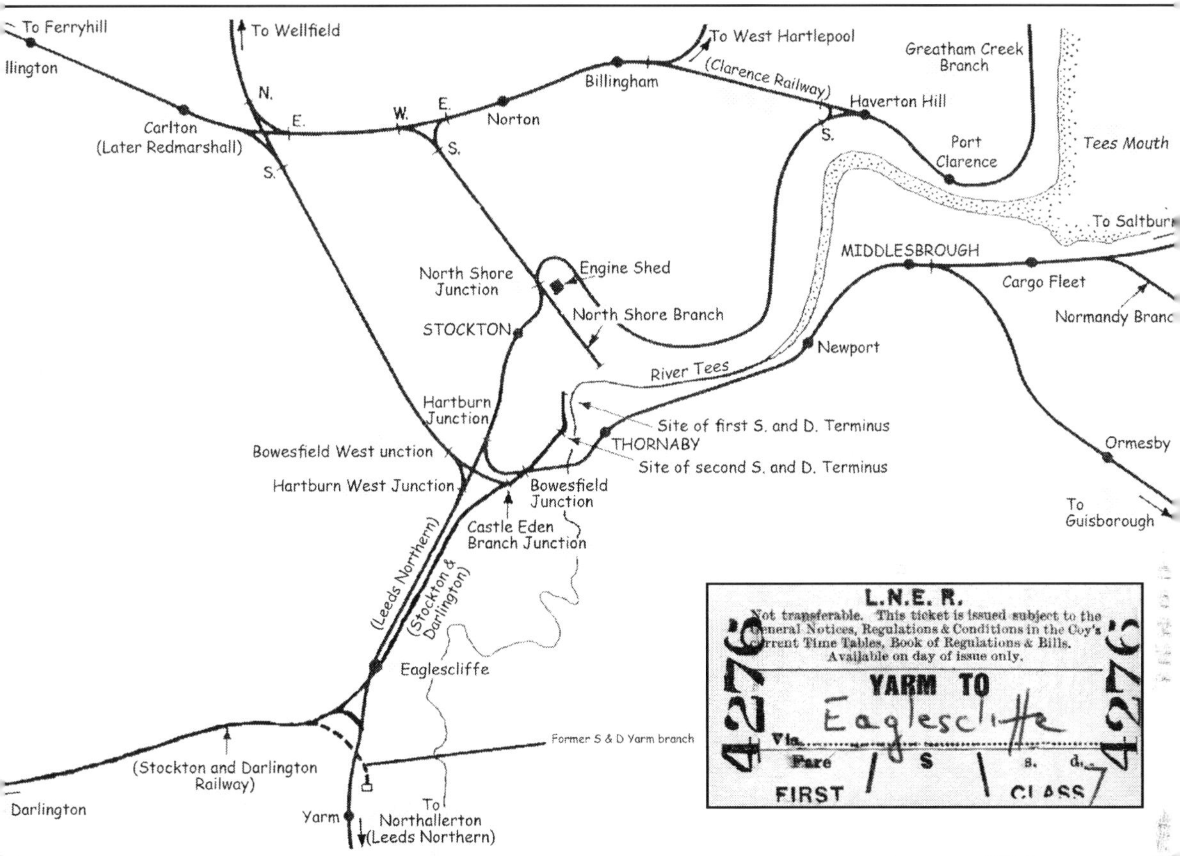

Stockton MPD

110. The last day of operation for Stockton MPD (code 51E) was the 13th June 1959. In the line-up were classes J27, K1, O8, B1, J94, WD and 4MT 2-6-0. (F.W.Hampson)

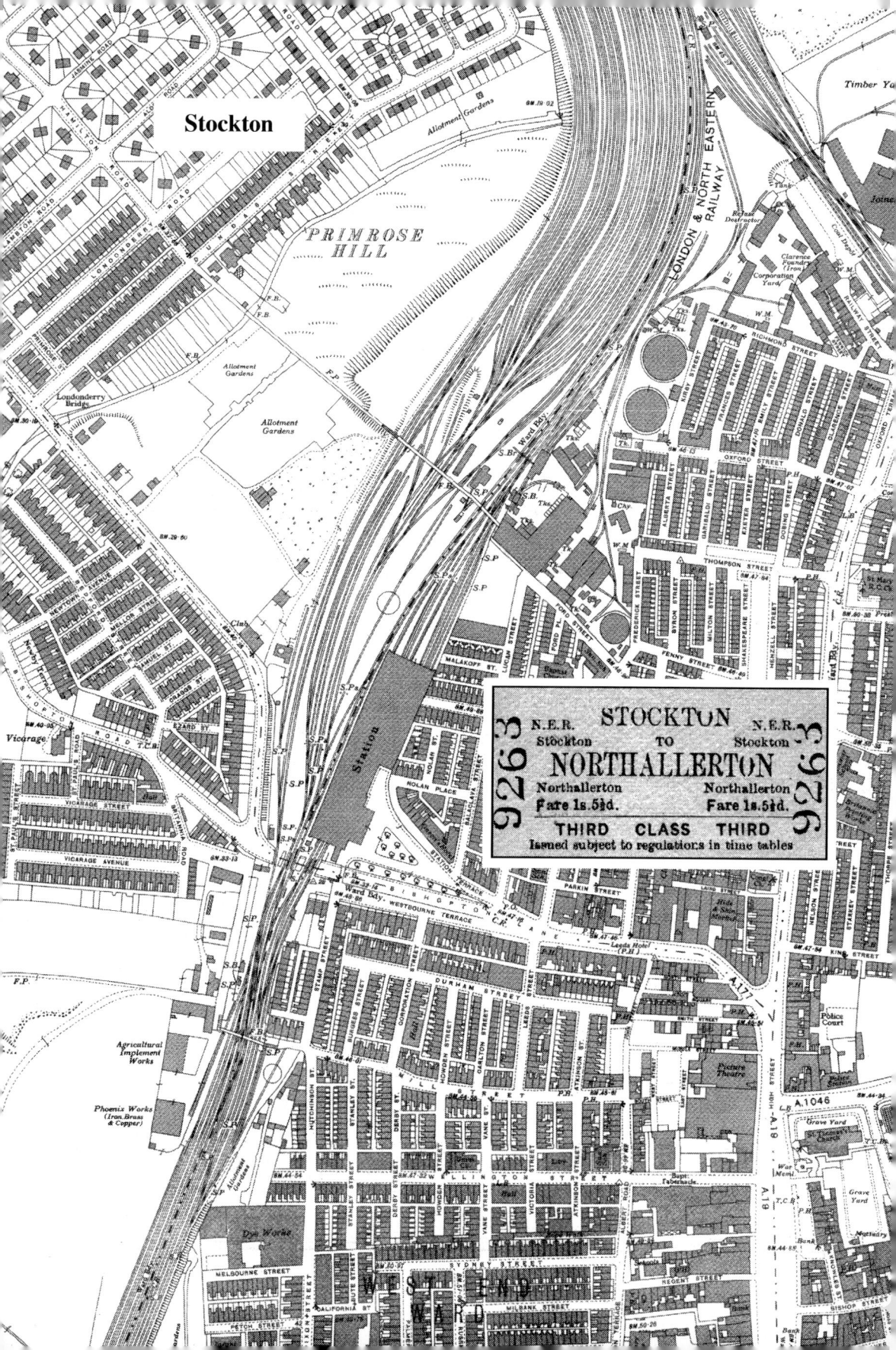

← XLII. Stockton-on-Tees station is seen here in 1939. It is served currently by Northern Trains operating between Middlesbrough/Whitby and Hartlepool/Sunderland/Newcastle.

Although it was not served by the S&DR, the current station was opened by the Leeds Northern Railway on 25th May 1852. It was renamed North Stockton shortly afterwards and at various times as Stockton North and Stockton North Shore. (The nearby station of Thornaby was known as South Stockton during this time.) The former was renamed Stockton-on-Tees on 1st November 1892 and was renamed plain Stockton in 1985.

111. The exterior of Stockton station on 25th May 1974. The station was opened in 1852 as Stockton-on-Tees. The rather fine building was built in 1898 and the present station's basic status reflects the influence of Middlesbrough and the decline of Stockton. (Colour-Rail.com)

112. On 7th July 1962, V1 class 2-6-2T no. 67639 is in the station with the 9.45am Middlesbrough to Newcastle parcels train. The station was still complete with two arches to the roof. The roof was removed as unsafe in 1979 and redundant platforms and sidings went at the same time.
(A.Brown/D.R.Dunn coll.)

113. The interior of the station with V2 class 2-6-2 no. 60905 on an express with ex-LMS coaches. This is possibly a Cross Country 11.00 departure. The V2 class was a very successful mixed traffic class. Being introduced just before WWII these locomotives coped with all that was thrown at them. This one served from April 1940 to September 1963. (A.Brown/ARPT)

114. Bishopton Lane signal box is on the left and a class 45 1-Co-Co-1 diesel is in the station. The building has lost one of its arches but there is still a wide range of goods sidings in the former Stockton North Yard. (J.Spencer Gilkes/Colour-Rail.com)

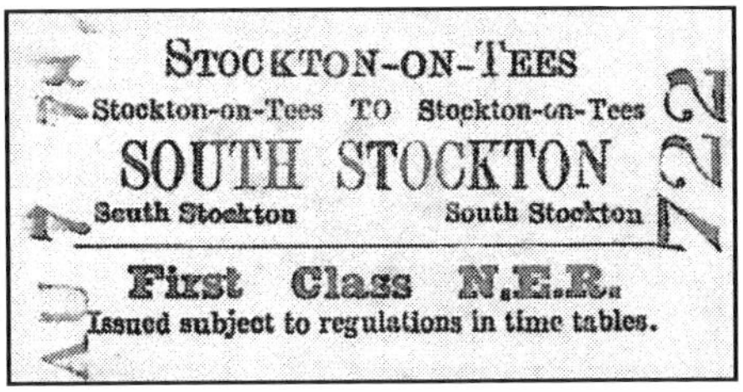

115. The Metropolitan-Cammell DMU had a headboard for Newcastle on 3rd September 1984 and the station has lost both its overhead roofs. (R.Humm coll.)

116. By 1st September 2021 the station buildings and footbridge have been moved down the platform and the station buildings have been turned into rather pleasant apartments. (D.A.Lovett)

117. A view from the station bridge with Grand Central High Speed Train nos 43465 and 43468 travelling non-stop to Sunderland on 9th June 2011. Grass has grown over the sidings. (R.R.Darsley)

118. The sidings on the 8th September 1962 were full of wagons attended by no. D3876 class 08 0-6-0DE and class 24 BoBoDE no. D5112 plus brake tender. Brake tenders were used to give weight and braking power to diesel locomotives hauling heavy, loose fitted, coal or ore trains. T.J. Thompson's scrap yard is in the left distance. Some steam and diesel locomotives were dismantled here. (A.Brown/ARPT)

119. From the 1830 S&DR branch from Stockton to Middlesbrough coal drops, the spread of sidings and depots along the Tees grew over the years until it culminated in the Tees Marshalling Yard. Here is the view of the up-marshalling yard on 15th August 1963 taken from the up tower. In the background are the landmarks of Tees Newport lifting bridge and the Middlesbrough Transporter Bridge. In 2023 a planned removal of the yard was announced. (J.Boyes/NERA)

120. We end with Thomas Hair's sketch of the Middlesbrough branch coal drops. From a farm with a population of 130 in 1825, the first new railway town, planned by the S&DR, though built by a separate company, had reached a population of 7,431 by 1861.
(T.Hair/Tyne & Wear Archives and Museum Service)

EVOLVING THE
Vic Mitchell and Keith Smith
ULTIMATE RAIL ENCYCLOPEDIA
INTERNATIONAL

126a Camelsdale Road, GU27 3RJ. Tel:01730 813169
A-978 0 906520 B- 978 1 873793 C- 978 1 901706 D-978 1 904474
E - 978 1 906008 F - 978 1 908174 G - 978 1 910356

Our RAILWAY titles are listed below. Please check availability by looking at our website **www.middletonpress.co.uk**, telephoning us or by requesting a Brochure which includes our LATEST RAILWAY TITLES also our TRAMWAY, TROLLEYBUS, MILITARY and COASTAL series.

email:info@middletonpress.co.uk

A
Abergavenny to Merthyr C 91 8
Abertillery & Ebbw Vale Lines D 84 5
Aberystwyth to Carmarthen E 90 1
Alnmouth to Berwick G 50 0
Alton - Branch Lines to A 11 6
Ambergate to Buxton G 28 9
Ambergate to Mansfield G 39 5
Andover to Southampton A 82 6
Ascot - Branch Lines around A 64 2
Ashburton - Branch Line to B 95 4
Ashford - Steam to Eurostar B 67 1
Ashford to Dover A 48 2
Austrian Narrow Gauge D 04 3
Avonmouth - BL around D 42 5
Aylesbury to Rugby D 91 3
B
Baker Street to Uxbridge D 90 6
Bala to Llandudno E 87 1
Banbury to Birmingham D 27 2
Banbury to Cheltenham E 63 5
Bangor to Holyhead F 01 7
Bangor to Portmadoc E 72 7
Barking to Southend C 80 2
Barmouth to Pwllheli E 53 6
Barry - Branch Lines around D 50 0
Bartlow - Branch Lines to F 27 7
Basingstoke to Salisbury A 89 4
Bath Green Park to Bristol C 36 9
Bath to Evercreech Junction A 60 4
Beamish 40 years on rails E94 9
Beattock to Carstairs G 84 5
Bedford to Wellingborough D 31 9
Berwick to Drem F 64 2
Berwick to St. Boswells F 75 8
B'ham to Tamworth & Nuneaton F 63 5
Birkenhead to West Kirby F 61 1
Birmingham to Wolverhampton E253
Blackburn to Hellifield F 95 6
Blackburn to Skipton G 85 2
Bletchley to Cambridge D 94 4
Bletchley to Rugby E 07 9
Bluebell Railway G 90 6
Bodmin - Branch Lines around B 83 1
Bolton to Preston G 61 6
Boston to Lincoln F 80 2
Bournemouth to Evercreech Jn A 46 8
Bradshaw's History F18 5
Bradshaw's Rail Times 1850 F 13 0
Branch Lines series - see town names
Brecon to Neath D 43 2
Brecon to Newport D 16 6
Brecon to Newtown E 06 2
Brighton to Eastbourne A 16 1
Brighton to Worthing A 03 1
Bristol to Taunton D 03 6
Bromley South to Rochester B 23 7
Bromsgrove to Birmingham D 87 6
Bromsgrove to Gloucester D 73 9
Broxbourne to Cambridge F16 1
Brunel - A railtour D 74 6
Bude - Branch Line to B 29 9
Burnham to Evercreech Jn B 68 0
Buxton to Stockport G 32 6
C
Cambridge to Ely D 55 5
Canterbury - BLs around B 58 9
Cardiff to Dowlais (Cae Harris) E 47 5
Cardiff to Pontypridd E 95 6
Cardiff to Swansea E 42 0
Carlisle to Beattock G 69 2
Carlisle to Hawick E 85 7
Carmarthen to Fishguard E 66 6
Caterham & Tattenham Corner B251
Central & Southern Spain NG E 91 8
Chard and Yeovil - BLs a C 30 7
Charing Cross to Orpington A 96 3
Cheddar - Branch Line to B 90 9
Cheltenham to Andover C 43 7
Cheltenham to Redditch D 81 4
Chesterfield to Lincoln G 21 0
Chester to Birkenhead F 21 5
Chester to Manchester F 51 2
Chester to Rhyl E 93 2
Chester to Warrington F 40 6
Chichester to Portsmouth A 14 7
Clacton and Walton - BLs to F 04 8
Clapham Jn to Beckenham Jn B 36 7
Cleobury Mortimer - BLs a E 18 5
Clevedon & Portishead - BLs to D180
Consett to South Shields E 57 4
Cornwall Narrow Gauge D 56 2
Corris and Vale of Rheidol E 65 9
Coventry to Leicester G 00 5
Craven Arms to Llandeilo E 35 2
Craven Arms to Wellington E 33 8
Crawley to Littlehampton A 34 5
Crewe to Manchester F 57 4
Crewe to Wigan G 12 8
Cromer - Branch Lines around C 26 0
Cromford and High Peak G 35 7
Croydon to East Grinstead B 48 0
Crystal Palace & Catford Loop B 87 1
Cyprus Narrow Gauge E 13 0
D
Darjeeling Revisited F 09 3
Darlington Learnside Newcastle E 28 4
Darlington to Newcastle D 98 2
Dartford to Sittingbourne B 34 3
Denbigh - Branch Lines around F 32 1
Derby to Chesterfield G 11 1
Derby to Nottingham G 45 6
Derby to Stoke-on-Trent F 93 2
Derwent Valley - BL to the D 06 7
Devon Narrow Gauge E 09 3
Didcot to Banbury D 02 9
Didcot to Swindon C 84 0
Didcot to Winchester C 13 0
Diss to Norwich G 22 7
Dorset & Somerset NG D 76 0
Douglas - Laxey - Ramsey E 75 8
Douglas to Peel C 88 8
Douglas to Port Erin C 55 0
Douglas to Ramsey D 39 5
Dover to Ramsgate A 78 9
Drem to Edinburgh G 06 7
Dublin Northwards in 1950s E 31 4
Dunstable - Branch Lines to E 27 7
E
Ealing to Slough C 42 0
Eastbourne to Hastings A 27 7
East Croydon to Three Bridges A 53 6
Eastern Spain Narrow Gauge E 56 7
East Grinstead - BLs to A 07 9
East Kent Light Railway A 61 1
East London - Branch Lines of C 44 4
East London Line B 80 0
East of Norwich - Branch Lines E 69 7
Effingham Junction - BLs a A 74 1
Ely to Norwich C 90 1
Enfield Town & Palace Gates D 32 6
Epsom to Horsham A 30 7
Eritrean Narrow Gauge E 38 3
Euston to Harrow & Wealdstone C 89 5
Exeter to Barnstaple B 15 2
Exeter to Newton Abbot C 49 9
Exeter to Tavistock B 69 5
Exmouth - Branch Lines to B 00 8
F
Fairford - Branch Line to A 52 9
Falmouth, Helston & St. Ives C 74 1
Fareham to Salisbury A 67 3
Faversham to Dover B 05 3
Felixstowe & Aldeburgh - BL to D 20 3
Fenchurch Street to Barking C 20 8
Festiniog - 50 yrs of enterprise C 83 3
Festiniog 1946-55 E 01 7
Festiniog in the Fifties B 68 8
Festiniog in the Sixties B 91 6
Ffestiniog in Colour 1955-82 F 25 3
Finsbury Park to Alexandra Pal C 02 8
French Metre Gauge Survivors F 88 8
Frome to Bristol B 77 0
G
Gainsborough to Sheffield G 17 3
Galashiels to Edinburgh F 52 9
Gloucester to Bristol D 35 7
Gloucester to Cardiff D 66 1
Gosport - Branch Lines around A 36 9
Greece Narrow Gauge D 72 2
Guildford to Redhill A 63 5
H
Hampshire Narrow Gauge D 36 4
Harrow to Watford D 14 2
Harwich & Hadleigh - BLs to F 02 4
Harz Revisited F 62 8
Hastings to Ashford A 37 6
Hawick to Galashiels F 36 9
Hawkhurst - Branch Line to A 66 6
Hayling - Branch Line to A 12 3
Hay-on-Wye - BL around D 92 0
Haywards Heath to Seaford A 28 4
Hemel Hempstead - BLs to D 88 3
Henley, Windsor & Marlow - BLa C 77 2
Hereford to Newport D 54 8
Hertford & Hatfield - BLs a E 58 1
Hertford Loop E 71 0
Hexham to Carlisle D 75 3
Hexham to Hawick F 08 6
Hitchin to Peterborough D 07 4
Horsham - Branch Lines to A 02 4
Hull, Hornsea and Withernsea G 27 2
Hull to Scarborough G 60 9
Huntingdon - Branch Line to A 93 2
I
Ilford to Shenfield C 97 0
Ilfracombe - Branch Line to B 21 3
Ilkeston to Chesterfield G 26 5
Inverkeithing-Kirkcaldy-Thornton Jn G 91 3
Inverkeithing to Thornton Jct G 76 0
Ipswich to Diss F 81 9
Ipswich to Saxmundham C 41 3
Isle of Man Railway Journey F 94 9
Isle of Wight Lines - 50 yrs C 12 3
Italy Narrow Gauge F 17 8
K
Kent Narrow Gauge C 45 1
Kettering to Nottingham F 82-6
Kidderminster to Shrewsbury E 10 9
Kingsbridge - Branch Line to C 98 7
Kings Cross to Potters Bar E 62 8
King's Lynn to Hunstanton F 58 1
Kingston & Hounslow Loops A 83 3
Kingswear - Branch Line to C 17 8
L
Lambourn - Branch Line to C 70 3
Lancaster to Oxenholme G 77 7
Launceston & Princetown - BLs C 19 2
Leeds to Harrogate G 86 9
Leeds to Selby G 47 0
Leek - Branch Line From G 01 2
Leicester to Burton F 85 7
Leicester to Nottingham G 15 9
Lewisham to Dartford A 92 5
Lincoln to Cleethorpes F 56 7
Lincoln to Doncaster G 03 6
Lines around Newmarket G 54 8
Lines around Stamford F 98 7
Lines around Wimbledon B 75 6
Lines North of Stoke G 29 6
Liverpool to Runcorn G 72 2
Liverpool Street to Chingford D 01 2
Liverpool Street to Ilford C 34 5
Llandeilo to Swansea E 46 8
London Bridge to Addiscombe B 20 6
London Bridge to East Croydon A 58 1
Longmoor - Branch Lines to A 41 3
Looe - Branch Line to C 22 2
Loughborough to Ilkeston G 24 1
Loughborough to Nottingham F 68 0
Lowestoft - BLs around E 40 6
Ludlow to Hereford E 14 7
Lydney - Branch Lines around E 26 0
Lyme Regis - Branch Line to A 45 1
Lynton - Branch Line to B 04 6
M
Machynlleth to Barmouth E 54 3
Maesteg and Tondu Lines F 06 2
Majorca & Corsica Narrow Gauge F 41 3
Manchester to Bacup G 46 3
Manchester to Liverpool G 88 3
Mansfield to Doncaster G 23 4
March - Branch Lines around B 09 1
Market Drayton - BLs around F 67 3
Market Harborough to Newark F 86 4
Marylebone to Rickmansworth D 49 4
Melton Constable to Yarmouth Bch E031
Midhurst - Branch Lines of E 78 9
Midhurst - Branch Lines to F 00 0
Minehead - Branch Line to A 80 2
Monmouth - Branch Lines to E 20 8
Monmouthshire Eastern Valleys D 71 5
Moretonhampstead - BL to C 27 7
Moreton-in-Marsh to Worcester D 26 5
Morpeth to Bellingham F 87 1
Mountain Ash to Neath D 80 7
N
Newark to Doncaster F 78 9
Newbury to Westbury C 66 6
Newcastle to Alnmouth G 36 4
Newcastle to Hexham D 69 2
Newmarket to Haughley & Laxfield G 71 5
New Mills to Sheffield G 44 9
Newport (IOW) - Branch Lines to A 26 0
Newquay - Branch Lines to C 71 0
Newton Abbot to Plymouth C 60 4
Newtown to Aberystwyth E 41 3
Northampton to Peterborough F 92 5
North East German NG D 44 9
Northern Alpine Narrow Gauge F 37 6
Northern Spain Narrow Gauge E 83 3
North London Line B 94 7
North of Birmingham F 55 0
North of Grimsby - Branch Lines G 09 8
North Woolwich - BLs around C 65 9
Nottingham to Boston F 70 3
Nottingham to Kirkby Bentinck G 38 8
Nottingham to Lincoln F 43 7
Nottingham to Mansfield G 52 4
Nuneaton to Loughborough G 08 1
O
Ongar - Branch Line to E 05 5
Orpington to Tonbridge B 03 9
Oswestry - Branch Lines around E 60 4
Oswestry to Whitchurch E 81 9
Oxford to Bletchley D 57 9
Oxford to Moreton-in-Marsh D 15 9
P
Paddington to Ealing C 37 6
Paddington to Princes Risborough C819
Padstow - Branch Line to B 54 1
Peebles Loop G 19 7
Pembroke and Cardigan - BLs to F 29 1
Peterborough to Kings Lynn E 32 1
Peterborough to Lincoln F 89 5
Peterborough to Newark F 72 7
Plymouth - BLs around B 98 5
Plymouth to St. Austell C 63 5
Pontypool to Mountain Ash D 65 4
Pontypridd to Merthyr F 14 7
Pontypridd to Port Talbot E 86 4
Porthmadog 1954-94 - BLa B 31 2
Portmadoc 1923-46 - BLa B 13 8
Portsmouth to Southampton A 31 4
Portugal Narrow Gauge E 67 3
Potters Bar to Cambridge D 70 8
Preston & Lancaster - BLs around G 82 1
Preston to Blackpool G 16 6
Preston to the Fylde Coast G 81 4
Preston to Lancaster G 74 6
Princes Risborough - BL to D 05 0
Princes Risborough to Banbury C 85 7
R
Railways to Victory C 16 1
Reading to Basingstoke B 27 5
Reading to Didcot C 79 6
Reading to Guildford A 47 5
Redhill to Ashford A 73 4
Return to Blaenau 1970-82 C 64 2
Rhyl to Bangor F 15 4
Rhymney & New Tredegar Lines E 48 2
Rickmansworth to Aylesbury D 61 6
Romania & Bulgaria NG E 23 9
Ross-on-Wye - BLs around E 30 7
Ruabon to Barmouth E 84 0
Rugby to Birmingham E 37 6
Rugby to Loughborough F 12 3
Rugby to Stafford F 07 9
Rugeley to Stoke-on-Trent F 90 1
Ryde to Ventnor A 19 2
S
Salisbury to Westbury B 39 8
Salisbury to Yeovil B 06 0
Sardinia and Sicily Narrow Gauge F 50 5
Saxmundham to Yarmouth C 69 7
Saxony & Baltic Germany Revisited F 71 0
Saxony Narrow Gauge D 47 0
Scunthorpe to Doncaster G 34 0
Seaton & Sidmouth - BLs to A 95 6
Selsey - Branch Line to A 04 8
Settle to Carlisle G 89 0
Sheerness - Branch Line to B 16 2
Sheffield towards Manchester G 18 0
Shenfield to Ipswich E 96 3
Shildon to Stockton G 79 1
Shrewsbury - Branch Line to A 86 4
Shrewsbury to Chester E 70 3
Shrewsbury to Crewe F 48 2
Shrewsbury to Ludlow E 21 5
Shrewsbury to Newtown E 29 1
Sirhowy Valley Line E 12 3
Sittingbourne to Ramsgate A 90 1
Skegness & Mablethorpe - BL to F 84 0
Slough to Newbury C 56 7
South African Two-foot gauge E 51 2
Southampton to Bournemouth A 42 0
Southend & Southminster BLs E 76 5
Southern Alpine Narrow Gauge F 22 2
South London Line B 46 6
South Lynn to Norwich City F 03 1
Southwold - Branch Line to A 15 4
Spalding - Branch Lines around E 52 9
Spalding to Grimsby F 65 9 6
Stafford to Chester F 34 5
Stafford to Wellington F 59 8
St Albans to Bedford D 08 1
St. Austell to Penzance C 67 3
St. Boswell to Berwick F 44 4
Stourbridge to Wolverhampton E 16 1
St. Pancras to Barking D 68 5
St. Pancras to Folkestone E 88 8
St. Pancras to St. Albans C 78 9
Stratford to Cheshunt F 53 6
Stratford-u-Avon to Birmingham D 77 7
Stratford-u-Avon to Cheltenham C 25 3
Sudbury - Branch Lines to F 19 2
Surrey Narrow Gauge C 87 1
Sussex Narrow Gauge C 68 0
Swaffham - Branch Lines around F 97 0
Swanage to 1999 - BL to A 33 8
Swanley to Ashford B 45 9
Swansea - Branch Lines around F 38 3
Swansea to Carmarthen E 59 8
Swindon to Bristol C 96 3
Swindon to Gloucester D 46 3
Swindon to Newport D 30 2
Swiss Narrow Gauge C 94 9
T
Talyllyn 60 E 98 7
Tamworth to Derby F 76 5
Taunton to Barnstaple B 60 2
Taunton to Exeter C 82 6
Taunton to Minehead F 39 0
Tavistock to Plymouth B 88 6
Tenterden - Branch Line to A 21 5
Three Bridges to Brighton A 35 2
Tilbury Loop C 86 4
Tiverton - BLs around C 62 8
Tivetshall to Beccles D 41 8
Tonbridge to Hastings A 44 4
Torrington - Branch Lines to B 37 4
Tourist Railways of France G 04 3
Towcester - BLs around E 39 0
Tunbridge Wells BLs A 32 1
U
Upwell - Branch Line to B 64 0
Uttoxeter to Macclesfield G 05 0
Uttoxetor to Buxton G 33 3
V
Victoria to Bromley South A 98 7
Victoria to East Croydon A 40 6
Vivarais Revisited E 08 6
W
Walsall Routes F 45 1
Wantage - Branch Line to D 25 8
Wareham to Swanage 50 yrs D 09 8
Watercress Line G 75 3
Waterloo to Windsor A 54 3
Waterloo to Woking A 38 3
Watford to Leighton Buzzard D 45 6
Wellingborough to Leicester F 73 4
Welshpool to Llanfair E 49 9
Wenford Bridge to Fowey C 09 3
Wennington to Morecambe G 58 6
Westbury to Bath B 55 8
Westbury to Taunton C 76 5
West Cornwall Mineral Rlys D 48 7
West Croydon to Epsom B 08 4
West German Narrow Gauge D 93 7
West London - BLs of C 50 5
West London Line B 84 8
West Somerset Railway G 78 4
West Wiltshire - BLs of D 12 8
Weymouth - BLs A 65 9
Willesden Jn to Richmond B 71 8
Wimbledon to Beckenham C 58 1
Wimbledon to Epsom B 62 6
Wimborne - BLs around A 97 0
Wirksworth - Branch Lines to G 10 4
Wisbech - BLs around C 01 7
Witham & Kelvedon - BLs a E 82 6
Woking to Alton A 59 8
Woking to Portsmouth A 25 3
Woking to Southampton A 55 0
Wolverhampton to Shrewsbury E 44 4
Wolverhampton to Stafford F 79 6
Worcester to Birmingham D 97 5
Worcester to Hereford D 38 8
Worthing to Chichester A 06 2
Wrexham to New Brighton F 47 5
Wroxham - BLs around F 31 4
Y
Yeovil - 50 yrs change C 38 3
Yeovil to Dorchester A 76 5
Yeovil to Exeter A 91 8
York to Scarborough F 23 9